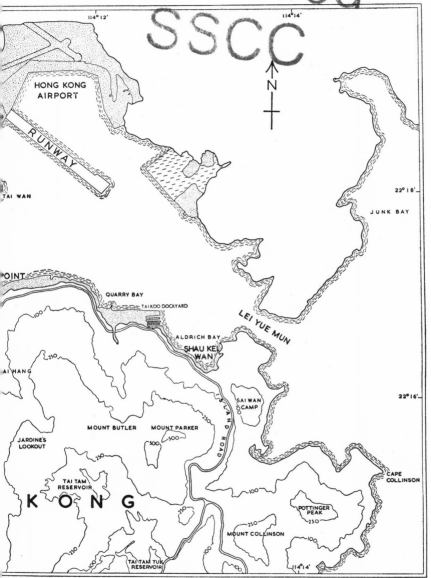

FRAGRANT HARBOUR

Armorial bearings were presented to Hong Kong on behalf of Her Majesty the Queen by H.R.H. the Prince Philip, Duke of Edinburgh, when he visited the Colony in March, 1959. The crest consists of a royal lion wearing the imperial crown and holding a pearl, representing Hong Kong as the 'Pearl of the Orient.' The shield carries pictures of a naval crown symbolising the Colony's link with the Navy and Merchant Navy, battlements indicating the Battle of Hong Kong in 1941, and two Chinese junks to indicate trade on the seas surrounding the Colony. A royal lion and Chinese dragon support the shield and crest, symbolising the British and Chinese aspects of the Colony. They stand on a green mount surrounded by water, an allusion to Hong Kong Island.

FRAGRANT HARBOUR

A Short History of Hong Kong

By

G. B. ENDACOTT

and

A. HINTON

GREENWOOD PRESS, PUBLISHERS
WESTPORT, CONNECTICUT

Library of Congress Cataloging in Publication Data

Endacott, G   B
    Fragrant harbour.

    Reprint of the ed. published by Oxford University
Press, Hong Kong.
    Bibliography: p.
    Includes index.
    1. Hongkong—History. I. Hinton, A., 1920–
joint author. II. Title.
ₑDS796.H757E5 1977ₗ   951'.25   76–57678
ISBN 0–8371–9456–3

© *Oxford University Press, 1962*

Preface

In this book we have aimed at presenting a brief account of the growth of Hong Kong from somewhat humble beginnings into the modern teeming industrial and commercial centre that it now is. We have tried to present the history as an essay in material and cultural contacts between East and West and as the unfolding of the story of improving human relationships within a framework of commercial and industrial enterprise under an administration which has aimed at safeguarding the interests of all sections of the community. While modern Hong Kong is largely the product of the post-war years, there are many facets of its life which are a product of its history and we hope that the following pages will help the general reader and visitor to a better understanding of present day Hong Kong and its problems.

At the end of each chapter there are extracts of source material which have been chosen to give a contemporary flavour to the times and the people described in the narrative.

G. B. ENDACOTT
A. HINTON

Hong Kong
January, 1962.

Acknowledgements

The authors wish to thank the Hong Kong Government for permission to reproduce the armorial bearings of the Colony; the Librarians at the Colonial Secretariat and Supreme Court for the use of library facilities by courtesy of the Departments concerned; the Information Services Department for supplying much of the material used for illustrations, and the Commissioner of Police and the Crown Lands and Survey Office of the Public Works Department for information supplied. The Crown Lands and Survey Office also kindly drew the maps.

They are grateful to the Department of Geography and Geology at the University for assistance with illustrations; to the Librarian of the Hong Kong University Library, Mr. J. M. Braga, Mr. Chung King-pui, M.B.E., J.P., Mr. Chiu Tse-nang, the Shell Company, Jardine, Matheson & Company, the 'Star' Ferry Company, the Hong Kong & Yaumati Ferry Company and others who helped to supply information upon which this book is partly based; to Mr. Peter Ng and Mr. Wen Ch'ing-hsi for supplying Chinese characters and to Mr. Wen and Mr. J. M. Braga for reading the script and making various suggestions.

Contents

LIST OF ILLUSTRATIONS

CHAPTER I

The Significance of Hong Kong

THE SIZE OF HONG KONG

Hong Kong is a small British colony on the south-east coast of China. Its total area is slightly under 400 square miles, made up of the island of Hong Kong (29 square miles), the Kowloon peninsula (3¼ square miles) and the New Territories which consist of a comparatively large mainland area north of Kowloon and of 235 islands, large and small, near to it (365½ square miles). This is not, of course, very impressive compared with the 4,135,000 square miles of neighbouring China, or the 3,000,000 square miles of the United States of America or even the 94,000 square miles of Great Britain.

What is then the significance of the history of such a small area? The history of any district is always important to itself, for the traditions of a place, its way of life, its approach to its problems, its social and political emotions, all come from the past. But the history of Hong Kong, although very brief, has a greater importance than local tradition.

THE MEETING OF EAST AND WEST

In Hong Kong can be seen on a small scale the meeting of East and West, the mixing of two very different traditions. The problems which arise from contact between two races of completely different stock and outlook, between two different civilizations, these can be seen in Hong Kong. The history of the Colony is to some extent a record of misunderstanding between races, sometimes more intense, sometimes less intense, but gradually diminishing as the races learn to respect each other, to understand each other and to co-operate.

This process of growing co-operation is still continuing, and Hong Kong is one of the few areas where Chinese and western Europeans are in daily and usually quite friendly contact with each other.

It may be objected that the Europeans of Hong Kong have not generally been representative of the people of Europe, for the wanderers are in some respects always different from those who stay at home. It can also be said that the Chinese who at different periods have left their native villages and towns to come to the foreign settlement of Hong Kong are not typical of the Chinese. It remains true, however, that in Hong Kong men of Chinese tradition and men of European tradition have been in continuous contact with each other for over a century.

LACK OF HISTORICAL REMAINS

Hong Kong was not deserted when the Europeans came and so its history goes back beyond their coming, but its importance in history really begins only with their arrival. Since it has such a short history it is lacking in those ancient remains which add so much to the interest of history. Moreover much of what was built in the early days of the establishment of Hong Kong as a British colony has now been demolished, so but few remains exist which date back even to the nineteenth century. Nevertheless, a wealth of information about the development of the Colony can be gathered from the names of streets, districts and buildings, which bear the names of previous governors, other officials and many private individuals. The name of every Governor is commemorated in the names of streets or buildings, from Pottinger Street, named after the first Governor, to the Sir Robert Black Training College, named after the Governor appointed in 1958. The name of Elliot, the first administrator of Hong Kong, is not now commemorated, but previously the road called Glenealy bore his name—Elliot Vale.

In its short history, Hong Kong illustrates much of what has been happening in the world in the past 120 years. In the story of Hong Kong can be seen the development of international trade, the spread first of Western power and then of Western ideas, the growth of population, the changing means of transport, the development of industry and other technological advances, the spread of education, improvements in medicine, and the gradual improvement of relations between men of different races and different traditions. The history of Hong Kong, therefore, has an importance which is out of proportion to its geographical area.

Extract from Harold Ingrams, Hong Kong, *London, 1952.*

The idea was always that in Hong Kong you should buy and sell with whom you liked, where you liked, when you liked and what you liked. Nature had helped by endowing it with a natural harbour which was the only deep-sea harbour between Singapore and Shanghai. It was the entrance to China for trade from Europe, the Middle East, India and Malaysia. As the world has developed so has the position of Hong Kong improved. It holds not only a strategic position on the steamship routes of the world but now on the main air routes as well.

Extract from the report in the Hong Kong Daily Press *of 21st February 1923 of a speech by Dr. Sun Yat-sen to the students of Hong Kong University, 20th February 1923.*

Dr. Sun Yat-sen who received another ovation on rising to speak, began by saying that he felt as though he had returned home, because Hong Kong and its university were his intellectual birthplace. He had not prepared a speech but thought he would like to answer certain questions which had been put to him many times and which, no doubt, many

3

present would also like to put to him. He had never before been able to answer it properly, but he felt to-day that he was in a position to answer. The question was 'Where and how did I get my revolutionary and modern ideas?'. The answer was, 'I got my ideas in this very place; in the Colony of Hong Kong'. 'I am going to tell you,' continued Dr. Sun, 'how I got those ideas. More than thirty years ago I was studying in Hong Kong and spent a great deal of spare time in walking the streets of the Colony. Hong Kong impressed me a great deal, because there was orderly calm and because there was artistic work being done without interruption. I went to my home in Heungshan twice a year and immediately noticed the great difference. There was disorder instead of order, insecurity instead of security. When I arrived home I had to be my own policeman and my own protector. The first matter for my care was to see my rifle was in order and to make sure plenty of ammunition was still left. I had to prepare for action for the night. Each time it was like this, year after year. I compared Heungshan with Hong Kong and, though they are only 50 miles apart, the difference of the Government impressed me very much. Afterwards, I saw the outside world and I began to wonder how it was that foreigners, that Englishmen could do such things as they had done, for example, with the barren rock of Hong Kong, within 70 or 80 years, while China, in 4,000 years, had no place like Hong Kong.'

Without good government a people could do nothing and in China 'we had no government' and were miserable for many centuries. 'Immediately after I graduated I saw,' added Dr. Sun, 'that it was necessary to give up my profession of healing men and take up my part to cure the country. That is the answer to the question, where did I get my revolutionary ideas: it is entirely in Hong Kong.'

They were still fighting for good government and as soon as they had good government the Chinese people would be contented and peaceful. That much could be proved by

4

Hong Kong and the Straits Settlements, for there were over one million Chinese in the South, and about 600,000 here, and whatever they might have been before they went to such places, they were now peaceful and good citizens. The Chinese people were easily governed and with good government would be content. Dr. Sun concluded with these words:

'My fellow students; you and I have studied in this English Colony and in an English University and we must learn by English examples. We must carry this English example of good government to every part of China'.

CHAPTER II

The West Comes to China

LACK OF CONTACT BETWEEN THE EAST AND THE WEST

China has a long history. Much even of the more modern part of that history is uncertain; of the earliest part we can get only glimpses through ancient legends and more recently through a number of archæological discoveries.

For most of this long history there was no direct contact between the West and China. In Roman times, even before the beginning of the Christian era, there was certainly indirect trade, if not direct contact, between the Roman dominions and the Han Empire in China. Silk passed along the Silk Route of Central Asia from China to the eastern shores of the Mediterranean Sea, and was much in demand in Rome. Yet, despite this quite considerable trade, the West knew nothing very definite about China and China knew nothing about the West.

Roman power collapsed, the Dark Ages followed in Europe and in turn gave way to the Middle Ages, but still China and Europe remained strangers to each other. Yet during the T'ang dynasty (618–907), two religions—a form of Christianity known as Nestorian Christianity and Islam—spread into China, showing that there were movements of people and ideas between West and East.

THE MONGOL EMPIRE

While Europe was changing, so too was China which saw the rise and fall of dynasties, internal rebellion and external wars, decay and reform. At one period in the thirteenth century China was conquered by the Mongols and for nearly a century was ruled by them. During this period, associated with the names, known even in Europe, of Genghis Khan 成吉思汗 and Kublai Khan 忽必烈, a wide variety of foreigners came to China. The vast Mongol Empire stretched from Russia to the China Sea. To China, the richest part of this huge empire, came travellers from Central Asia, the Middle East, the Near East and Europe.

MARCO POLO

Those from Europe were few in number, a few priests and a few merchants about most of whom we know very little, but the record of one of these merchants, Marco Polo, was quite widely read in Europe and for the first time made Europe really conscious of China. This new-found knowledge of China did not have any immediate effect, but it remained in the imagination of Europe. Later, in the late fifteenth century and in the sixteenth century, it played an important part in stimulating the European voyages of discovery to the Far East and to the West. The Portuguese led the way but they were soon followed by the Spaniards, the Dutch, the English and the French, while the Russians pushed their way overland towards the boundaries of China.

THE PORTUGUESE

The Portuguese reached India by sea in 1498. They advanced to Malacca, which they seized in 1511, and in 1513 they reached China. After some years of uncertainty, for some of them were not liked by the Chinese authorities owing to their apparent arrogance and lawlessness, they were permitted to settle at Macao in 1557, where they have remained until today.

THE JESUITS

Before long representatives of other European nations were also coming to trade with China, and not only to trade. Roman Catholic missionaries tried from the early days of

7

European expansion to the Far East to enter China. The Jesuit, Francis Xavier, tried to do so shortly before his death in 1552, and it was not long before some Jesuit priests under the auspices of the Portuguese Government succeeded not only in reaching Peking but in having considerable influence there. The most famous of these were the Italian Matteo Ricci (in China from 1583 to 1610), the German Adam Schall (1622–66) and the Belgian Ferdinand Verbiest (1659–88). Their influence was largely due to their knowledge of mathematics and astronomy and for many years it was a Jesuit who was director of the Board of Astronomy under the Ch'ing dynasty. Although there were attempts to preach Christianity and although the Jesuits did for a long time hold a privileged position in Peking, most of the Europeans who went to China went there for trade.

THE GROWTH OF TRADE

Throughout the seventeenth and eighteenth centuries the trade slowly increased. It was, however, considerably limited by Chinese restrictions and particularly by the fact that China did not need the goods of Europe. The European merchants had, therefore, to pay for most of their purchases in silver and their governments were much opposed to this export of silver. Europe imported silk and tea in particular, but the eighteenth century saw also a considerable vogue in Chinese artistic products and Chinese decorations. Thus in the palace at Schönbrunn, on the outskirts of Vienna, Queen Maria Theresa of Austria had two rooms furnished entirely in the Chinese manner, with Chinese furniture, tapestries and ornaments.

THE IMPORTANCE OF ENGLAND

By the end of the eighteenth century the leading country trading with China was England. This was partly because of her growing commercial and political control in India, from the ports of which many British ships sailed on to China, but mainly because of the popularity of tea in England. British trade with China was until 1833 in the hands of the East India Company, which had a monopoly of the trade between Britain and the Far East.

Though Britain was the most prominent of the countries trading with China, there were nationals of many other Western countries who carried on regular and profitable trade with that kingdom. The Portuguese from their settlement at Macao, the Dutch from their bases in the East Indies, the French, the Americans, were all trading with China before the end of the eighteenth century, and ships from other countries were not an uncommon sight in Chinese waters.

TRADING CONDITIONS

What were the conditions under which trade was carried on between China and these Western countries? Firstly, the trade was limited to Canton. Other Chinese ports were closed to the Western merchants. The trading season, for reasons of the winds which facilitated the coming and going of sailing ships, was limited to the months from October to May, and only during those months could foreigners live in the Canton district. Even then they were not allowed to live in, or even to enter, the city of Canton but had to stay in a particular area outside the city in what were known as their 'factories'.

Their freedom was still further limited, at least in theory and sometimes in practice, by regulations which forbade them to learn Chinese, to employ Chinese servants, to use sedan chairs, to possess fire-arms, or to have their wives with them. These restrictions were irksome but not unbearable, especially as they were not always enforced.

Other restrictions, which interfered with trade, were regarded as far more serious. The European merchants had come there to trade, to buy from China goods which they could sell at a profit in the West and to sell to China other

9

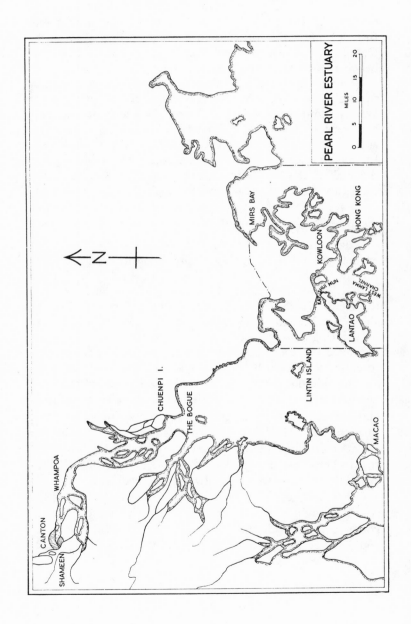

PEARL RIVER ESTUARY

goods, also at a profit. They were prepared to put up with restrictions of their comfort and convenience, but they were less patient about restrictions on the trade itself.

THE CO-HONG 公行

It was bad enough being limited to one port, but even in that port they were not allowed freedom of trade with all merchants. They could trade only with one group of merchants, the Co-Hong. This severely limited their ability to bargain and to secure the best prices for their goods. They felt that if they had been free to go to any merchants they liked they could have sold at higher prices and bought at lower prices than they could when dealing with one body only. Moreover, since the Co-Hong merchants had to pay large sums of money to the Imperial Court in return for their monopoly, they took every opportunity to try to secure large profits from the foreign merchants. In addition, the foreign merchants had to pay customs duties and harbour dues which were not fixed but varied considerably and often seemed to them excessive.

THE FAILURE OF WESTERN EMBASSIES

The Western merchants constantly complained about these trading restrictions. To add to their discontent was the knowledge that they were regarded as barbarians and that they were allowed even this limited amount of trade on sufferance. The trade could be stopped at any time.

Though they were far from their native countries these merchants seemed to have no great fear for their personal safety, but they were concerned about the precarious nature of their trade. They wanted more trading facilities and less uncertainty about the continuance of the trade. Various official embassies were, therefore, sent to Peking to try to secure better relations between the Western merchants and the Chinese authorities. A British embassy went to Peking in 1793, a Dutch embassy followed two years later, a Russian one in 1806 and another British one, led by Lord Amherst, in 1816. These attempts at negotiation failed because the Chinese Court refused to recognize that any other country could be regarded in any way as the equal of China.

THE ATTITUDE OF CHINA

The attitude of China was clear. Foreigners had come to China to trade. China did not need their goods but she was willing to trade with other countries on her own terms. By consenting to trade at all she was doing the foreigners a great favour. If they did not like the conditions imposed by the Chinese authorities, they were always free to leave.

Moreover, the Chinese naturally measured civilization by a Chinese yard-stick. People who did not behave in the Chinese way were not civilized. So the foreigners, with their strange tongues and different habits and customs, were obviously barbarians and should therefore be treated as inferiors. The behaviour of some of the merchants and sailors from the West did not always show the West at its best and did not help to dispel the Chinese feeling of superiority.

THE ATTITUDE OF WESTERN MERCHANTS AND OFFICIALS

The traders from Western countries did not share the Chinese belief that they were inferior to the Chinese; on the contrary, they were often guilty of thinking that they were superior and the Chinese inferior. They based this belief partly on the greater technical advances made in the West, where the Industrial Revolution was developing, and partly on the natural habit of people to regard the ways they know and follow as superior to those that are strange to them. Furthermore, and this was most important, the Westerners could not understand the unwillingness of the Chinese Government to permit trade to be carried on more freely.

12

Surely trade was good for all. It enabled each country to exchange the goods of which it had a surplus for others which it could not produce itself. The Westerners were only too willing to buy silk and tea from China and to supply China, as far as they could, with whatever she needed. Why then were the Chinese so obstinate in their refusal to expand trade, so unwilling to throw open their ports to the Western merchants? The Chinese merchants themselves seemed willing to trade, so why was the government so unco-operative?

THE INCREASE OF TRADE

Despite all restrictions, however, trade between China and the West did increase steadily. For long the foreign merchants had to pay for many of their purchases in silver, for there were few goods which China was willing to accept. Western governments were not at all pleased with this drain of silver from their own countries to the Far East. The merchants were therefore eager to find some commodity which the Chinese were willing to buy from them. When such a commodity was found, trade did increase quite rapidly.

Unfortunately this increase of trade made the Western merchants still more conscious of the trading restrictions; their removal would make possible the still greater expansion of trade and the still greater increase of profits. Even more unfortunate was the fact that the commodity which enabled the trade to increase was opium, a drug which, though of medicinal value when used properly under a doctor's orders, is most unhealthy and dangerous when its use is not controlled.

THE OPIUM TRADE

Opium was not introduced into China by the Western traders. It had long been used as a medicinal drug and from the early seventeenth century the habit of smoking it had gradually spread. At first the supply of opium was home-grown, but later a lot of it was imported from India. Since the British had gained control of much of India by the end of the eighteenth century, the opium trade fell largely into British hands. The cultivation of the poppy, from which opium is derived, brought much revenue to the government of Bengal.

The opium trade was at first quite small but in the nineteenth century it increased rapidly. Early in the eighteenth century the annual import of opium into China was about 200 chests. A chest of opium varied in weight according to the province from which it came but contained on the average about 120 pounds. By the beginning of the nineteenth century the import had increased to about 5,000 chests a year; by 1831 it was 16,500 chests. Until this time trade between Britain and China and British India and China had been in the hands either of the East India Company itself or of 'country traders' licensed by the Company. This had somewhat limited the trade, but in 1833 the monopoly was abolished. As a result more traders could engage in commerce with the Far East and there was a considerable increase in trade. Thus in the 1838–9 season nearly 40,000 chests of opium were imported for sale to the Chinese.

THE IMPORTING OF OPIUM FORBIDDEN

The Chinese Government had early realized that the smoking of opium was a dangerous habit and had become gravely concerned about the spread of the habit. It had, therefore, passed edicts forbidding the smoking of opium. These proved useless so in 1800 the import of opium was forbidden. The trade in opium was therefore illegal. It still remained profitable, however, for Chinese merchants were willing to co-operate with the foreign merchants, buying their opium from them and smuggling it into China. This was done with the knowledge and help of many of the Chinese officials themselves who, in return for 'gifts', were prepared to permit the trade.

For the British merchants it was simply a matter of profit. If they supplied the opium which Chinese merchants were willing to buy from them they would make large profits; if they did not supply it merchants of other countries would step in and make the profits. The fact that the Chinese Government had forbidden the trade did not worry them since that government seemed unable to stop its own subjects from co-operating in the trade.

That opium was a drug, the use of which could weaken and even destroy men, did not seem to concern them very much. In England itself the same voices which abolished slavery were raised in protest against the opium trade, but they were not strong enough to compel the British Government to take any action. So the trade increased. A debate on the opium trade was held in the House of Commons in 1843, and had the opponents of the trade been better organized they might have passed a motion condemning it. Unfortunately they failed.

The merchants themselves were concerned with profits, not with morals. If they could continue to sell opium to Chinese merchants and make a profit, they would not concern themselves overmuch with the use and effects of the opium. They convinced themselves that it was no business of theirs what use was made of the opium after they had sold it.

UNFORTUNATE EFFECTS OF THE CHINESE FEELING OF SUPERIORITY

Had the Chinese authorities been willing to allow more trade in other directions, the opium trade might not have grown so large. Had the Chinese Government been willing to regard the British Government as an equal and to receive its representative as the ambassador of an equal state instead of as the messenger of an inferior state coming to pay homage to the Emperor, the British Government might have been

15

willing to help to stop the smuggling activities of its subjects. Since, however, other trade was severely limited, the foreign merchants took advantage of the Chinese demand for opium and the failure of the Chinese authorities to prevent its import. The British Government was not allowed to negotiate on equal terms with the Peking Government, and so it did nothing to control its merchants.

Brief extracts from a letter from the East India Company to Lord Amherst, 17th January 1816, as he set out on his embassy to Peking.

. . . We shall, therefore, only recapitulate shortly . . . the principal aggressions of which the Supra-Cargoes complain, and the remedies which appear to be requisite.

First. Under the head of aggressions are to be noted.

1st   The attempt of the local authorities of Canton in the year 1813, to interfere in the case of Mr. Roberts with the Company's nomination of managers of their Affairs, and, in effect, to introduce a principle which would make the sanction of the Government necessary to such nomination, and go to place the whole of the European Trade with that Empire, under their control.

2ndly   Another attempt of one of the Authorities in the same year, to establish what is termed the System of Co-Hong; that is, to confine the Company's Dealings and the whole European Trade of Canton, to two or three Native Merchants, who would thus have the power of regulating the prices of purchases and sales, or in other words a strict Monopoly.

3rdly   Prohibiting in the year 1814, the Natives of China from serving in the English Factory, and from communication with the Supra-Cargoes.

4thly   Seizing, beating, and imprisoning the Chinese Linguist, who had been employed by the Supra-Cargoes, on the ground of his . . . connection with them; and even reporting him to the Emperor to be engaged in treasonable practices with them.

5thly Returning the Address of the Supra-Cargoes to the Canton Authorities unopened.

7thly The local Authorities in the Edicts promulgated by them, used very offensive language towards the Supra-Cargoes; and in their personal behaviour towards them, were contemptuous and insulting . . .

8thly The conduct of the Local Government at length became so hostile as to render it, in the judgment of the Supra-Cargoes, their duty to proceed themselves to the suspension of the British Trade.

Extracts from a translation of a letter from the Viceroy Loo 盧坤 *to the Hong Merchants at Canton, 18th August 1834.*

To refer to England—should an official personage from a foreign country proceed to the said nation, for the arrangement of any business, how could he neglect to have the object of his coming announced, in a memorial to the said nation's King? or how could he act contrary to the requirements of the said nation's dignity, doing his own will and pleasure?

Since the said barbarian Eye states that he is an official personage, he ought the more to be thoroughly acquainted with these principles.

Before, when he offered a letter, I, the Governor, saw it inexpedient to receive it; because the established laws of the celestial Empire do not permit Ministers, and those under authority, to have private intercourse by letter with outside barbarians, but have hitherto, in commercial affairs, held the merchants responsible. . . . There has never been such a thing as outside barbarians sending in a letter. . . .

. . . I have thrice issued orders, which the said merchants were required to make themselves acquainted with, and to enjoin. The several subjects discussed in their several orders, are the long established regulations, well known to all barbarian merchants of every nation who have business at Canton . . . Obey, and remain! Disobey, and depart! There are no two ways.

CHAPTER III

The Opium War and the Cession of Hong Kong

LORD NAPIER'S MISSION

In the early part of the nineteenth century the foreign merchants trading to Canton wished to increase their trade with China; the Chinese Government wished to limit that trade. The foreign merchants were importing increasing amounts of opium into China; the Chinese Government had prohibited this. Such a situation seemed certain to cause trouble.

The British Government was being pressed by the merchants, whose influence was strengthened by newly-formed merchants' organizations, to help increase trade with China. The abolition of the monopoly of the trade held by the East India Company was a step in this direction. As a further step the British Government sent Lord Napier to the Far East in 1834 as Chief Superintendent of Trade.

Lord Napier was to have general control over the British merchants, and he was to try to establish direct relations with the Chinese Government officials. It was hoped that he might be able to have some of the restrictions on trade removed and some grievances settled. If these were discussed in a friendly spirit, arrangements satisfactory to both China and the Western countries could surely be made. He was to urge the British merchants to be careful not to offend the Chinese by ill-considered actions and to remember 'the duty of conforming to the laws and usages of the Chinese Empire'.

IMPOSSIBILITY OF DISCUSSIONS ON A BASIS OF EQUALITY

This attitude seems reasonable, but Lord Napier's mission failed for one fundamental reason—he could not talk on an equal basis with officials of the Chinese Empire because he was regarded as inferior. There could, in the opinion of the Chinese, be no equality of status between Britain and China. The British merchants were tolerated but they were not to be given further facilities for trade; they could trade only on the conditions laid down by the Chinese authorities. If they did not like this they could go away.

INFLUENCE OF THE BRITISH MERCHANTS ON THEIR GOVERNMENT

Such an attitude hurt the pride of a nation which certainly did not regard itself as inferior. Moreover, the British Government was influenced in its attitude by the opinions of those on the spot, i.e. the merchants who were trading with China. These, of course, were pursuing their own interests, and they had powerful support among the merchants in England, whose influence in Parliament had greatly increased following the reform of Parliament in 1832.

War between Britain and China was not inevitable but it was a real possibility. Many of the merchants thought that Britain should use force to compel China to adopt a more liberal attitude towards trade with the West. After all, trade would benefit China as well as Britain.

THE COMPLETE FAILURE OF LORD NAPIER'S MISSION

If he had possessed more knowledge of Chinese regulations and customs and if he had been better advised, it is possible that Napier's mission might have met with some success. In fact it was a complete failure. His attempt to start discussions led to a stoppage of trade, and the sending of two British warships to Canton to protect British merchants there made matters worse. The Chinese authorities distrusted him, calling him 'barbarian eye' and describing him as 'laboriously vile'. Before long, Napier, now sick with fever, had to leave Canton and withdraw to Macao, where he died in October 1834. He was succeeded as Chief Superintendent first by J. F. Davis, his chief assistant, and then in January 1835, by Sir George Robinson. Robinson left in December 1836, and was succeeded by Captain Charles Elliot, R.N.

THE MERCHANTS' PETITION TO THE BRITISH GOVERNMENT, 1834

To Britain it appeared that an attempt at friendly discussion had been met by insult to the representative of the King. In a petition to the British Government in December 1834, the British merchants in Canton suggested that matters would have been very different if Napier had been given fuller powers and backed by force. This opinion now began to gain support in Britain. Even many who were not at all concerned with trade disliked the Chinese attitude of superiority and influential religious opinion condemned their refusal to admit Christian missionaries. But China was a long way from Britain, and however important these questions might appear to the merchants in Canton and Macao and their associates in Britain they were not generally regarded as burning questions by other people.

THE APPOINTMENT OF LIN TSE-HSU 林則徐

Meanwhile, after Napier's withdrawal from Canton, trade had been resumed and the smuggling of opium—with the co-operation of the Chinese local authorities—continued to increase. Imperial edicts had failed to stop it. As the evil increased it became ever more imperative to make a determined effort to stop opium from entering the country. This effort was undertaken when Lin Tse-hsu was appointed as special Imperial Commissioner for the suppression of the opium trade and sent to Canton in 1839.

Lin Tse-hsu had started his administrative career almost twenty years earlier and had gained a high reputation as a just and humane man and an efficient official. From 1832 to 1837 he had been Governor of Kiangsu and had then been promoted to the post of Governor-General of Hupeh and Hunan. While holding this post he sent a memorial to the throne on the subject of opium, stressing the need for drastic laws against its use. He proposed and put into effect in his own provinces a programme of destroying the equipment of smokers, of setting a time-limit for smokers to reform, and of severe punishment of dealers and smugglers of opium. As a result he was summoned to Peking and after several audiences with the Emperor he was appointed Imperial Commissioner with full powers to deal with the opium question in Canton.

THE INITIAL ATTITUDE OF THE WESTERN MERCHANTS TOWARDS LIN

Commissioner Lin arrived in Canton in March 1839. The foreign merchants did not view his coming with any great alarm. They expected him to make things rather difficult for them for a short time, but they thought that this would be the prelude to bargaining about the rewards he should be given for allowing the trade to continue. The trade was valuable enough to bear the payment of heavy rewards of this kind and the European merchants in China were not unused to such dealings. It did not, however, take them long to realize their mistake and to recognize that in Lin the Emperor had a servant who was both efficient and determined to carry out the task entrusted to him.

THE SURRENDER OF OPIUM

Commissioner Lin acted quickly. On 18th March 1839, only eight days after his arrival in Canton, he ordered the foreign merchants to give up all their opium. He also insisted that they should individually sign a bond promising not to import any opium in future on pain of death. Until the opium was given up sixteen of the merchants were to be handed over as hostages. In the meantime the Western merchants were virtually imprisoned in the factories. Their Chinese servants were withdrawn, though they loyally saw that their employers were well supplied with food before they left.

The British Superintendent of Trade, Captain Elliot, went from Macao to Canton and attempted to negotiate with Lin, finally agreeing to the surrender of all the opium in British hands. This led to some difficulty for much of the opium did not belong to the merchants who were merely acting as the agents for others. Elliot promised, however, that the British Government would take the responsibility for all the opium belonging to British people which was destroyed. More than 20,000 chests of opium were handed over and Lin went to great trouble to make sure that it really was destroyed by mixing it with lime and sea water.

LIN'S SURPRISE AT THE BRITISH REACTION

Though Elliot would not agree to the bond which Lin had wanted the merchants to sign, the British were now free to leave or to carry on trade with their other goods. Opium, though important, had never been the only article of trade. Lin apparently thought that now the opium trade had been checked other trade would continue peacefully. He was, therefore, very surprised when the British withdrew to Macao and when he learned that Elliot had asked for military intervention.

Lin's point of view was that Western merchants were permitted to trade at Canton under certain conditions. By importing opium, they had been disregarding imperial edicts. Now an honest commissioner had forced the surrender of

23

their contraband and was preventing them from carrying on their illegal trade. But they were still able to carry on their legitimate trade under the same conditions as before, and Lin could not understand why they did not do so. Other merchants, less concerned with opium, seemed willing to carry on, so why not the British?

BLOW TO BRITISH PRESTIGE

On the British side, the action of Lin in virtually holding the foreign community to ransom until the merchants surrendered their opium seemed a blow to British prestige. The British had lost face. To the merchants this offered an opportunity to persuade the British Government to use force in order to secure greater privileges of trade for them. It would be hard to defend the opium trade, particularly as there were many opponents of it in England itself, but to protect British citizens abroad was a different matter.

The British felt that the proper procedure would have been for Lin to seize the opium from the merchants and then to have prosecuted the smugglers in the courts. Instead, Lin had seized the opium by threatening the whole community but had taken no legal action against the offending merchants. To Westerners unacquainted with China this seemed very high-handed and the London representatives of the China merchants were able to press for strong action by the British Government to protect the merchants.

THE BEGINNING OF HOSTILITIES

The British did not feel safe at Macao because Lin threatened to attack them there. The Portuguese, for their part, did not wish to become involved in any trouble between the Chinese and the British. The British community therefore embarked on merchant ships and moved to Hong Kong harbour, there to await the arrival of a British expedition and the settlement of the dispute.

The killing of Lin Wei-hi 林維喜, a Chinese villager, in a shore quarrel in July 1839, made relations between the British and the Chinese authorities still worse. Elliot paid some compensation to the man's family and, though he was not able to find out who the guilty person was, he tried those concerned and some of them were sentenced to imprisonment in England. He would not, however, hand any of these men over to Lin to be punished by the Chinese authorities. The Chinese now attempted to destroy the British ships by fire-rafts and so hostilities began.

ACTION BY THE BRITISH GOVERNMENT

When news of the events at Canton reached England, the Government felt that it had to take some action against China. The fact that the goods which Lin had seized consisted of opium, an illegal import into China, did not affect the matter as far as the British Government was concerned. What was important was that British merchants had been imprisoned in their factories, had been forced under threats to surrender their goods, and that an attempt had been made to extract a promise from them and from the British Superintendent of Trade that there would be no trade in opium in the future.

British merchants trading to the Far East had long been agitating for greater facilities, for the freedom to trade with more ports in China, for the removal of the various restrictions on trade and for permission to do business with any Chinese merchants they chose. Lord Palmerston, Foreign Secretary in the Government of Lord Melbourne, decided to send an expedition which would settle this matter of trade once and for all. He would secure the safety of British merchants trading with China by a treaty. This treaty should either arrange for the cession of an island to secure British subjects against future interference, or give guarantees that trade would be conducted under satisfactory conditions. The expedition sent was not to attempt any major attack on China.

25

The aim was to use sufficient force to make economic measures, such as the blockading of the rivers and coast and the Grand Canal, more effective, and by this economic pressure to induce the Chinese to accept the British demands.

OPIUM REGARDED BY THE CHINESE GOVERNMENT AS THE SOLE CAUSE OF THE WAR

To the Chinese authorities the crux of the matter was opium. The wider question of general trade relations was not regarded as particularly important. The Western merchants came of their own free will to trade and the Chinese Government allowed them to trade under certain conditions. The Westerners had to an increasing extent imported opium, though that was illegal. When at last the Chinese officials had taken determined action to stop them from doing so the British Government sent an armed expedition to support the merchants. The British Government insisted on the merchants being indemnified for the opium destroyed. It refused to forbid its merchants to engage in the opium trade, on the grounds that it was the responsibility of the Chinese to prevent the import of opium. These facts strengthened the Chinese view that the war was being fought about opium.

THE EMOTIONAL LEGACY OF THE QUARREL

This association of the Anglo-Chinese war with the opium trade has unfortunately affected Anglo-Chinese relations ever since, though it is now quite irrelevant. Western influence and Western techniques were spreading to all parts of the world in the nineteenth century, and the wars with China, whatever their immediate causes, form part of this general expansion of influence. The emotional attitude of many Chinese towards Europeans in general and the British in particular is affected even today by the Opium War. In just the same way the emotional attitude of many English people towards the Spaniards was for a long time affected by stories of the Spanish Inquisition and the Armada, and that of many Americans towards the British by the Stamp Act.

THE CONVENTION OF CHUENPI 穿鼻

In June 1840, the British took the offensive, an expedition sailing north from Macao, but hostilities were not continuous and often ceased for negotiations. War was not declared and to some extent trade continued through the Americans. Elliot, the British plenipotentiary, was conciliatory and at one point came to an agreement with Keshen (Ch'i-shan 琦善), who represented the Chinese. As a result of this agreement, known as the Convention of Chuenpi, Hong Kong was occupied by a British naval force on 26th January 1841. Finally, however, neither government accepted this Convention.

ELLIOT REPLACED BY POTTINGER

Because Elliot was regarded as too conciliatory he was replaced by Sir Henry Pottinger who arrived at Macao in August 1841. He pursued the campaign energetically and a year later, on 29th August 1842, when faced with the possibility that Nanking might be captured, the Chinese agreed to the Treaty of Nanking which ended the war.

THE TREATY OF NANKING, 1842

By this treaty the British gained compensation for the opium which had been destroyed by Commissioner Lin in 1839, while the Chinese also had to pay the costs of the British expedition. The ports of Amoy, Foochow, Ningpo and Shanghai were to be opened to British trade, in addition to Canton. British consuls and other British subjects could live in these places. Moreover the Co-Hong was to be abolished and British merchants could trade with any Chinese merchants they liked. It was also agreed that a 'fair and regular' tariff for exports and imports should be fixed.

The British also secured the diplomatic equality which they had been eager to get for so long, while a good measure of security was obtained by the cession of the island of Hong Kong. This would provide a base from which British traders could be given protection, and also a port where ships could be overhauled and repaired, and a centre from which British subjects on the China Coast could be controlled.

THE ANNEXATION OF HONG KONG

This treaty was ratified in June 1843, and then Hong Kong was officially declared a British colony with Sir Henry Pottinger as its first Governor. The British had in fact been in possession of it for two years already, but this had been a military occupation during hostilities and the British Government had been unwilling to recognize it as a permanent occupation. The men on the spot saw that Hong Kong could afford security to the merchants, but those in England saw it chiefly as an added responsibility which they did not welcome. Eventually the British Government followed the advice of the men who were on the spot.

COMMISSIONER LIN

Commissioner Lin had been appointed Governor-General of Kwangtung and Kwangsi early in 1840. As the British expedition, however, began to gain successes in the war, Lin lost favour with the Emperor who now blamed him for the outbreak of hostilities. In September 1840, he was dismissed and had to return to Peking in disgrace to await his punishment. His place was taken by Keshen who had been the chief Chinese representative in the discussions with Elliot. Though Lin was thus demoted, he gradually rose again into favour for he was a very able man. By the time he died in 1850 he was again a leading official of the Imperial Government.

Extract from a letter from Lord Palmerston addressed to the Minister to the Emperor of China, 22nd February 1840.

. . . But the British Government demands full satisfaction from the Government of China for these things. In the first place it requires that the ransom which was exacted as the price for the lives of the Superintendent, and of the imprisoned merchants, shall be restored to the persons who paid it, and if . . . the goods themselves, which were given up to the Chinese Authorities . . . cannot be restored to their owners . . . then the British Government demands and requires that the value of those goods shall be paid back by the Government of China to the British Government, in order that it may be paid over to the Parties entitled to receive it.

In the next place, the British Government demands satisfaction from the Government of China for the affront offered to the Crown of Great Britain, by the indignities to which Her Majesty's Superintendent has been subjected; and the British Government requires that in future the Officer employed by Her Majesty to watch over the commercial interests of Her subjects in China, shall be treated and shall be communicated with by that Government, and by its officers, in a manner consistent with the usages of civilized nations, and with the respect due to the dignity of the British Crown.

Thirdly . . . The British Government demands security for the future, that British Subjects resorting to China for the purposes of trade, in conformity with the long-established understanding between the two Governments, shall not again be exposed to violence and injustice while engaged in their lawful pursuits of commerce. For this purpose, and in order that British Merchants trading to China may not be subject to the arbitrary caprice either of the Government at Peking, or its local authorities at the seaports of the Empire, the British Government demands that one or more sufficiently large and properly situated islands on the coast of China, to be fixed upon by the British Plenipotentiaries, shall be permanently given up to the British Government as a place of residence and of commerce for British subjects, where their persons may be safe from molestation, and where their property may be secure. . . .

CHAPTER IV

Relations with China, 1842-1961

THE TREATY OF NANKING

Hong Kong was occupied by the British on 26th January 1841, following the Convention of Chuenpi. It was not, however, officially ceded until the Treaty of Nanking which was signed in August 1842 and ratified in the following June. As related in the previous chapter, the Chinese Government paid compensation to the British, opened four additional ports at which British subjects could reside and trade, promised that the tariff should be settled by mutual agreement, and recognized the diplomatic equality of Britain with China. The importance of this last factor is difficult to exaggerate.

Chromolithograph by Sir H. Darell

Conference at Chusan, 1840

DIPLOMATIC INEQUALITY AS A CAUSE OF THE WAR

The difficulties which had caused the war might have been settled peacefully if China had recognized the principle of diplomatic equality, the idea that nations should discuss difficulties between them as equals. But China had regarded herself—and in view of her history not unnaturally—as superior to all other nations. She could not, therefore, allow them to meet her on equal terms. So, whenever the West had tried to come to an agreement with her, she had regarded the representative of the Western country as a bearer of gifts, paying tribute to the great central kingdom, craving favours and perhaps to be given certain concessions. She had never regarded a Western official as one who could discuss matters on equal terms or who had any right to make complaints.

RECOGNITION OF EQUALITY

Now the situation was different. As a result of defeat in war, China had been forced to recognize that militarily the West was strong and could not be defied without trouble. Britain had insisted on being recognized as an equal. Henceforth, if any question arose between the two countries it would be discussed on this basis of equality, unwillingly conceded by China as a result of the military and naval strength of the West. Perhaps it would be truer to say that any question would still be decided on a basis of inequality, but whereas the power had previously rested in the hands of China, it now lay in the hands of the Western countries. They were able, increasingly as the century wore on, to use their superior power to gain concessions from China. Diplomatic equality gave rise to the treaties which were later called 'unequal'.

THE INCOMPLETENESS OF THE TREATY OF NANKING

The recognition of diplomatic equality explains why several important matters, which had contributed to the ill-feeling and disputes out of which the war had arisen, were not dealt with in the treaty. The treaty ended the war and gave certain minimum concessions to Britain; having got those minimum concessions, Britain was willing to leave the other matters for later settlement. There was no need to prolong the war until every detail had been settled, for China had now accepted the principle of negotiation and had suffered a demonstration of British power.

THE TREATY OF THE BOGUE 虎門仔

Among the matters left undecided by the Treaty of Nanking were the questions of opium, the treatment of foreigners accused of crimes, the details of the tariff, regulations for the conduct of trade, and the extent to which concessions won by the British would have to be granted to other foreigners also. Discussions on these matters were held and several of them were dealt with in the supplementary Treaty of the Bogue, signed in October 1843.

OPIUM

The Treaty of the Bogue, like that of Nanking, did not deal with the question of opium. The official attitude of the British Government was that this was not a matter for discussion. The Chinese Government had every right to declare the trade illegal and was fully entitled to stop opium being landed in China, but the British Government should not help the Chinese to enforce their own laws. Unless the British Government itself passed laws forbidding the opium trade, no British official could help China stop the smuggling of opium. This negative attitude of the British Government towards the opium trade reflects the influence of the merchants of Hong Kong, who were selling opium to China, and of the authorities in British India, who gained much revenue from the opium harvest.

33

EXTRA-TERRITORIALITY

Extra-territoriality was established by the Treaty of the Bogue and it later gave rise to great indignation, yet it was not a new or unfair device. If people of one country were tried and punished according to the totally different laws and customs of another country, serious trouble might be caused. Extra-territoriality helped to maintain order while avoiding such trouble. In the Middle Ages in Europe it was not unusual for people from one state to enjoy extra-territorial rights in another. Venetian traders living in the English port of Southampton possessed such rights, which allowed them to be tried by their own people according to their own laws. In the treaty ports of China, extra-territoriality almost certainly assisted in keeping order. The British, for instance, were quite ready to punish those of their own people who committed crimes there, but they would not have been prepared to hand them over to the Chinese authorities for trial and punishment according to Chinese law. Thus many were punished who might otherwise have been assisted to escape.

CHINESE GOVERNMENT RESENTMENT

It was natural that the Chinese Government should resent the British authorities who had forced them to make so many concessions. These concessions could not be refused, but the Chinese did not co-operate very willingly with those who had extorted them. The Chinese officials discouraged their citizens from moving to Hong Kong and so, for some years, though labourers went there, few of the Chinese who ranked higher in the social scale moved to the new colony.

CONCILIATORY ATTITUDE OF THE BRITISH GOVERNMENT

The British Government on the other hand seemed anxious to develop good relations with China. Bad relations would serve only to restrict trade and to make the life of a Westerner in the treaty ports rather less happy than it might otherwise be, and rather less safe. Therefore the British did make some effort, though not bound to do so by any treaty, to stop the opium trade in Hong Kong. As a result all the opium supply ships moved away for a short time in 1843.

This policy did not last long, however, for other nations were also involved in the trade and would soon have taken the place of the British. Indeed, the British merchants themselves would simply register their ships with other countries and go on bringing opium. Moreover, the Chinese themselves were still assisting the trade and there were very few Chinese officials who possessed the determination shown a few years earlier by Commissioner Lin in his efforts to prevent the import of opium.

PIRACY

The British desire to avoid any trouble with the Chinese Government is shown also in the attitude towards piracy. Trade suffered a good deal from piracy but the British authorities for some time took no real action to try to root out the pirates. One strong reason for this was the fear that such action would offend the Chinese authorities. Action against the pirates should be taken by the Chinese officials and the British did not wish to interfere or to help enforce Chinese laws. There were other reasons also. The British Navy did not like such work as it brought no glory and, at this time, no prize money. Moreover the naval warships could not pursue the pirate vessels into shallow water as the later gunboats were able to do, and in any case it was extremely difficult to recognize a pirate unless he was caught in the act. It was not until 1849 that any determined attack was made on pirates by the British Navy, but in that year two pirate fleets were destroyed.

This really marks the point when the British Government decided to go its own way without worrying too much about official Chinese co-operation. Foreign trade with the Far East was increasing and 1849 marked the beginning of the period when Britain, almost alone, assumed responsibility for policing the Chinese coastal waters against pirates.

THE DESIRE OF WESTERN MERCHANTS FOR MORE CONCESSIONS

The British—and other Westerners who by this time had gained similar concessions to those granted to the British—were dissatisfied with the limits placed on their trade with China. In 1842 they had gained the right to trade at five treaty ports, to trade freely with any Chinese merchants there, and they had also secured a low tariff. But China was bigger than five ports and the Westerners would not be satisfied until they had the right to trade in all parts of China, to travel freely in that huge country. The appetite is stimulated by eating, according to a well-known French proverb; the appetite for trade with China was certainly stimulated by a taste of the profits to be made from that trade.

PRESSURE FROM MISSIONARIES

Pressure for the further opening of China to the West did not come solely from merchants. They had powerful allies in the missionaries. These were allowed to work only in the treaty ports. Many sincere Christians, however, felt that it was their duty to teach their religious convictions to all those who had not yet heard the word of God. To them it was wrong that they should not be allowed to preach Christianity to the untold millions in China who had never heard of Jesus. For these missionaries the opening of China would mean a tremendous opportunity to save the souls of the ignorant heathen. So, as was often the case in exploration and colonization in the nineteenth century, religion and trade went hand in hand, for the opening up of hitherto unknown lands to the Europeans gave opportunities to both traders and missionaries.

MINOR INCIDENTS BETWEEN CHINESE AND EUROPEANS

Apart from this general desire among many of the British people in Hong Kong and the treaty ports to see China opened further to Western penetration, there were several incidents which could easily become excuses for trouble. In Canton, for instance, there were frequent attacks on Europeans and there had been a dispute about the right of foreigners to reside there. Yeh Ming-shun 葉名琛 became the Chinese High Commissioner at Canton in 1852 and his attitude was unco-operative and contributed to ill-feeling. There was also a general feeling of unrest and insecurity about that time because of the T'ai P'ing 太平 rebellion. This rebellion, partly a peasant revolt and partly a movement for reform, was led by Hung Hsiu-ch'uan 洪秀全, a village schoolmaster who was greatly influenced by a mixture of vague and misunderstood Christian ideas and a belief in his own greatness. It aimed at establishing a new dynasty and its efforts to do so plunged the area of China around the lower Yangtse into civil war and confusion for many years. The rebels captured Nanking in 1854 and made it their capital. They were not suppressed until 1865 and then only with foreign help. In 1854 the Crimean War broke out and the possibility of a clash in the Far East between the forces of Britain and Russia added to the general unrest.

THE ARROW AFFAIR

In such circumstances a minor incident could easily be magnified and lead to a serious dispute, and that is what happened in 1856. In that year a small vessel, the Arrow, Chinese-owned but registered in Hong Kong and thus under the protection of the British flag, was boarded at Canton and the crew imprisoned on a charge of piracy. The British consul at Canton demanded an apology and the release of the crew. He was strongly supported by Bowring, then Governor of Hong Kong, who issued an ultimatum and when he did not get a satisfactory reply prepared to attack Canton. Bowring was strongly criticized in England for his action which was condemned by Parliament. Palmerston supported him, however, and in the General Election which followed the defeat of the Government, Palmerston was returned to power and war began.

THE SECOND ANGLO-CHINESE WAR

The French also joined in the war following the execution by the Chinese of a French missionary, Chapdelaine. The war went on longer than had been expected, owing largely to the diversion of a British expedition to India where the Indian mutiny against the British broke out in 1857. Early in 1858, however, Canton was captured and then an expedition was sent to the north. In the same year the Treaty of Tientsin brought the war to an end.

In 1860, British insistence that an envoy should go to Peking to ratify the treaty led to a renewal of the war. Peking was occupied and the Chinese were forced to sign the Convention of Peking, making certain additions to the Treaty of Tientsin.

THE TREATIES OF TIENTSIN AND PEKING

By these treaties of 1858 and 1860, several more ports were opened to Western trade and residence (see map on page 73). Furthermore, foreigners were now permitted to travel anywhere in China, Western ships to sail up the Yangtze River, and Christians to preach their religion. The Chinese Government gave up its opposition to the import of opium and made the trade legal. China paid an indemnity and ceded the Kowloon peninsula up to Boundary Street to Britain, thus adding part of the mainland to the Colony of Hong Kong.

Kowloon City as it was in 1899 *Chung King-pui*

THE CESSION OF KOWLOON

Between 1841 and 1858 British people had often landed in Kowloon, and at one stage some British and Americans had started to build houses there until stopped by the Governor, Davis (1844–8). Bowring (1854–9) considered the area as worthless to the Chinese but valuable to the British, and he was eager that it should be ceded. A riot at Tsim Sha Tsui in 1859 indicated that the lawlessness of the Chinese inhabitants of Kowloon might be dangerous to the existing Colony, while the use of the peninsula as a camping ground for the military expedition being prepared for the campaign of 1860 showed its value for the army. So in March 1860, it was leased in perpetuity by the British. A few months later, by the Convention of Peking of October 1860, Kowloon was ceded.

39

THE NARROWING OF THE POWERS OF THE GOVERNOR
OF HONG KONG

The cession of Kowloon was not the only way in which Hong Kong was affected by the war. For some years the officials in Hong Kong had gradually been losing their powers of control over British citizens in the treaty ports. The war led to a definite restriction of the Governor's powers. He ceased to be responsible for relations with China and he ceased also to be Superintendent of Trade, remaining simply Governor of the Colony, responsible for its good administration.

ANTI-BRITISH FEELING IN HONG KONG

A further effect of the war was the growth of ill-feeling between Chinese and British in Hong Kong. This was inevitable since Britain and China were at war with one another. In Canton the British factories were burnt down; at Whampoa the British wharves were destroyed. There was an unsuccessful attempt to stop food being brought to Hong Kong. Placards appeared on the walls in Hong Kong urging all Chinese to join in the struggle against the British. There was even a serious attempt in 1857 to poison the foreigners in the Colony by placing arsenic in the bread baked in an important Wanchai bakery! This led to the detention of many Chinese and the deportation of many more.

Even after the war a feeling of bitterness and insecurity remained, yet despite this the Chinese population in Hong Kong continued to grow. This was partly because the suffering caused by the T'ai P'ing rebellion, which was still continuing, caused many Chinese traders to seek security in Hong Kong. This influx led to increased trade which in turn attracted more immigrants.

THE CHINESE IMPERIAL MARITIME CUSTOMS

During the T'ai P'ing rebellion Shanghai was occupied by the rebel forces and the Chinese customs officials were unable to collect the customs duties. The European consuls began collecting the customs on behalf of the Chinese. This was found to be efficiently carried out and after the hostilities of the Second Anglo-Chinese War, the collection of customs at all the Treaty Ports was placed under the supervision of Europeans in the service of the Chinese Emperors, formed into a Chinese Imperial Maritime Customs service. It also dealt with light-houses, port installations and channels, and later assisted the Chinese Government with advice about foreign diplomatic relations.

THE HONG KONG BLOCKADE

Official relations with China were strained by the customs blockade which was enforced for nearly twenty years, from 1866 to 1886. During this period Chinese revenue vessels stopped and searched Chinese junks going from Hong Kong to the mainland. The opium trade had been made legal by the Treaty of Tientsin in 1858, but the Chinese Government had imposed a heavy tax on the import of opium, so smuggling was still profitable. The smuggled opium was usually carried from Hong Kong in Chinese junks. Sometimes even ships that were not bound for the Chinese mainland were stopped and searched and many protests were made by the Governors of Hong Kong about this blockade. Hong Kong merchants felt that it was an effort to lessen the growing importance of Hong Kong in the coastal trade and to lessen also the competition which Hong Kong was offering to the port of Canton.

THE END OF THE BLOCKADE

In 1876, following the murder of a British official on the distant border between Burma and Yünnan, the Chefoo 煙台 Convention was signed by Britain and China. By this, new ports were opened to foreign trade and a few other concessions made. It was also agreed that a commission should be set up to discuss the blockade. This commission, consisting of representatives of China and Britain, did not meet until 1886. Then an agreement was made for the control of the opium trade, and the customs blockade, which had not been enforced very much since 1882, was brought to an end. But smuggling did continue to a considerable extent, particularly across the Kowloon border, and so there were still some disputes.

THE GROWTH OF RUSSIAN AND FRENCH POWER IN THE FAR EAST

It seems strange that despite difficult relations with China there was never any fear that the Chinese might attack Hong Kong. Perhaps this was because of the little respect in which Chinese military power was held.

There was, however, considerable apprehension of Russia and France, for Britain was on bad terms with both countries and was uneasy at the growth of their power in the Far East. While Britain had been extending her influence in China, particularly in central China, Russia had been doing likewise in the north. In 1898 she secured a lease of the southern part of the Liaotung peninsula, including Dairen and Port Arthur. To counterbalance this Britain secured a lease of Weihaiwei, on the coast of Shantung.

In the south French power was growing. Already under Napoleon III she had gained control of Annam and Cochin-China, and following a war with China in 1884–5 she had occupied Tongking. In 1895 she had secured a little more territory, ceded by China to Annam, and priority rights in the development of the southernmost provinces of Yünnan, Kwangsi and Kwangtung. Moreover, in 1893 Russia and France had come together in an alliance.

THE LEASING OF THE NEW TERRITORIES

Britain felt uneasy about this alliance and about the growing power of each of these two states in the Far East. In order to be better able to defend Hong Kong if it should be attacked, she pressed for the possession of the area inland from Kowloon. This had been discussed by various British officials for several years. In June 1898, it was announced that the New Territories were leased as from 1st July 1898, for 99 years. It was not until April 1899 that they were actually taken over, and then only after some disagreement with the Chinese viceroy in Canton and a small amount of fighting with villagers in the New Territories themselves, at Kam Tin, Tai Po and Yuen Long for instance.

Hong Kong, the full Colony as it exists now, was thus complete—the island, Kowloon and the New Territories, including many adjacent islands. As to the number of these there has been great uncertainty and the number was in 1959 adjusted to 235.

For two years after the occupation of the New Territories there were disputes with the Chinese authorities about the exact boundaries, particularly over the Shum Chun area and Kowloon City. There was for a long time some uncertainty about the position of Kowloon City, because, though the Colonial Office definitely included it in the New Territories, Chinese opinion was that it did not form part of the lease.

Shell Company

A boundary stone at Sha Tau Kok, a village on the frontier between Hong Kong and China

THE BOXER REBELLION

Before the trouble over the lease of the New Territories had completely died down, relations with China were disturbed by the outbreak of the Boxer rebellion in 1899. As news of the attacks in the north of China, first on Chinese Christians and then on Europeans, reached Hong Kong, there was a certain amount of apprehension in the Colony, but in fact, though a number of Christians moved from China into the Colony, the South remained fairly quiet and Chinese Christians and Westerners in Hong Kong were quite safe.

OPPOSITION TO THE MANCHU DYNASTY

Another difficulty which threatened peaceful relations between Hong Kong and China arose from the growing opposition in the south of China to the Manchu dynasty. Thus in 1896 Sun Yat-sen 孫逸仙, the best known of Chinese reformers, was banished from the Colony because he was engaged in revolutionary activity against China. In the following years there was much support among Chinese resident in Hong Kong for the various reform movements, but the British Government refused to allow any official support to be given to any of the reformers, however much sympathy there might be with their aims.

LOANS TO CHINA

In the same period, towards the end of the nineteenth century and at the beginning of the twentieth century, the Colony was establishing ever closer links with China in financial matters, especially in making loans for railway development. There was no sentiment involved in the granting of these loans, which were purely business affairs, yet they did increase the interest of Britain and Hong Kong in the stability of China, and the interest of China in keeping on good terms with Hong Kong.

THE CHINESE REVOLUTION

The outbreak of revolution in 1911 and the overthrow of the Manchu dynasty again led to uncertainty in relations between Britain and China. The Revolution, like the T'ai P'ing rebellion, led to an influx of people into Hong Kong, but for the next few years China was far too busy with her own internal problems to worry very much about Hong Kong. Later, particularly as the Kuomintang Government of Chiang Kai Shek 蔣介石 spread its power, there came an increase in national feeling which led to difficulties between Britain and China.

The Chinese now became more and more critical of the unequal treaties, of extra-territoriality, of foreign rights, of foreign control of the Chinese customs. They demanded that the many privileges in the hands of foreign powers should be given up. In 1925 a boycott of British and Japanese goods was organized by the radical section of the Kuomintang 國民黨 party in Canton. This was followed almost immediately by an economic boycott of Hong Kong and a general strike by Chinese workers in the Colony. Essential services were maintained by the Army and Navy and the Volunteer Corps and before long the strikers began to drift back to work, but the boycott of British goods and shipping remained until October 1926.

THE JAPANESE WAR

Relations might easily have got worse in succeeding years, but soon the Kuomintang became occupied with extending its power to the North. Then came serious trouble between China and Japan. Already, as a result of war with China in 1894–5, Japan had established her influence in much of Korea, had gained Formosa, and had secured certain rights in China. Later, after the Russo-Japanese War of 1904–5, Japan was able to extend her influence into Manchuria. Her influence in China further increased during the First World War, 1914–8. In 1931 the Japanese seized Manchuria, creating the state of Manchukuo, and in 1932 attacked

Shanghai. Five years later full-scale war broke out between Japan and China, and the latter country, faced with this attempt at conquest, could not at the same time attack Western power in her territory.

THE SECOND WORLD WAR

Then came the outbreak of the Second World War in Europe in 1939 and two years later, on 8th December 1941, the Japanese suddenly attacked Hong Kong. By 25th December the Colony was captured and for the next three years and eight months Hong Kong was part of the Japanese Empire.

In August 1945, the Japanese were forced to surrender and once again the British took control of the government of Hong Kong. Though Britain and China had been allies in the war against Japan from the end of 1941 onwards, the Nationalist Government of China was by no means content to see Hong Kong pass once again under British control. Extra-territoriality had by this time come to an end, foreign concessions in China had been given up, and Hong Kong remained as the chief reminder of the days when China had been largely dominated by the foreigners.

THE CHINESE PEOPLE'S REPUBLIC

A new factor now appeared on the scene with the rapid growth of Communist power. By October 1949, the Communists had obtained sufficient success in the civil war against the Kuomintang Government to establish their own régime, the Chinese People's Republic. The advance of the Chinese Communist armies to the borders of the New Territories led to a feeling of uneasiness in Hong Kong, for it seemed by no means unlikely that they would wish to seize the Colony. No such attempt was made, however, and though there were a few border incidents no serious clash occurred.

The outbreak of the Korean War in 1950 between the North Korean Communist régime and the American-influenced republic in South Korea and the subsequent intervention in the war of Communist China led to an embargo on trade with China in a large number of strategic goods. This dealt a very heavy blow at the trade of Hong Kong with China. Hong Kong had to earn her living in other ways if she was to survive, and so there has come about the tremendous industrial development of the Colony.

Despite the embargo and international tension, relations between Hong Kong and her large neighbour have remained correct and the last few years have been surprisingly free from incident.

Extract from a translation of a letter to Queen Victoria from the High Commissioner Lin Tse-hsu appearing in the Chinese Repository, *February 1840.*

. . . Out of the wealth of our Inner Land, if we take a part to bestow upon foreigners from afar, it follows, that the immense wealth which the said foreigners amass ought properly speaking to be portion of our own native Chinese people. By what principle of reason then should these foreigners send in return a poisonous drug, which involves in destruction those very natives of China? Without meaning to say that the foreigners harbour such destructive intentions in their hearts, we yet positively assert that from their inordinate thirst after gain, they are perfectly careless about the injuries they inflict upon us, and such being the case, we should like to ask what has become of that conscience which heaven has implanted in the breasts of all men?

We have heard that in your own country opium is prohibited with the utmost strictness and severity—this is a strong proof that you know full well how hurtful it is to mankind.

A letter to Sun Yat-sen from the Colonial Secretary, 4th October 1897.

Sir,

In reply to your letter, undated, I am directed to inform you that the Government has no intention of allowing the British Colony of Hong Kong to be used as an asylum for persons engaged in plots and dangerous conspiracies against a friendly neighbouring Empire, and that in view of the part taken by you in such transactions, which you euphemistically term in your letter 'Emancipating your miserable countrymen from the cruel Tartar yoke', you will be arrested if you land in this Colony, under an order of banishment issued against you in 1896.

I have etc.

J. H. STEWART LOCKHART,
Colonial Secretary.

Extracts from a speech to the Hong Kong Legislative Council on the taking over of the New Territories, 11th October 1899, by Sir Henry Blake.

The months that have elapsed since my resumption of the Government have been months fraught with exceptional anxiety and responsibility. Under the Convention between Her Majesty the Queen and His Imperial Majesty the Emperor of China, the area of 29 square miles that has hitherto been the extent of the Colony was increased by a lease for ninety-nine years of an area of four hundred square miles with an estimated population of 100,000.

It was assumed that the knowledge of the just treatment of the Chinese inhabitants of Hong Kong and British Kowloon would induce the population of the leased area to accept the jurisdiction of Great Britain with equanimity if not with pleasure. Had it been possible to take over the possession immediately this assumption might have been verified. But there were unavoidable delays. . . .

48

Unhappily, the interval was taken advantage of by agitators who disturbed the minds of the people by statements that their lands would be forcibly taken from them, and their most cherished customs forbidden. The first symptoms of hostility were shown on the 31st March when the building of a matshed at Taipo-hu was prevented and the men engaged in erecting boundary posts were stopped from working. I saw the Viceroy on 2nd April at Canton and pointed out that if protection was not afforded to working parties and surveying parties, I could not adhere to my undertaking not to take over the Territory before the 17th. . . . What took place on the 15th of April and following days has already been laid before you. The resistance having been overcome I have endeavoured to satisfy the people that they may safely depend upon British justice, and that no man's property will be confiscated, and I have no doubt that the people will soon recognise this.

CHAPTER V

The Administration of Hong Kong

THE OCCUPATION OF HONG KONG

In January 1841, Captain Charles Elliot, the British Superintendent of Trade, had come to a preliminary agreement with Keshen at Chuenpi, by which Hong Kong was to be ceded to the British. On 26th January a British naval force landed at Possession Point. As we saw in Chapter III the Convention of Chuenpi did not become the basis of a treaty, and it was not until the ratification of the Treaty of Nanking in June 1843 that the British occupation was recognized as permanent. For the first two years of occupation, therefore, all arrangements made were temporary and makeshift.

THE ADVANTAGES OF HONG KONG

In April 1841, Lord Palmerston, the British Foreign Secretary, referred to Hong Kong as 'a barren island with hardly a tree on it'. By Elliot and other men in the Far East it was not viewed so slightingly. They saw that it possessed a fine harbour, and that it was admirably situated as a base for trade with China and as a naval base from which that trade could be defended. It was close to Canton, which was another advantage, for Elliot expected trade to remain centred in South China, especially Canton, as in the past. They also saw that it had a sufficient water supply—for how could they foresee the later difficulties which would arise in this respect? As a place of refuge it was ideal, for being small it could be easily defended.

Hong Kong was not uninhabited when it was first occupied by the British. Indeed, it had probably been inhabited from very early times judging from the pottery and stone implements discovered on Lantao Island and on Lamma Island. Little is known about these first inhabitants who were probably akin to those primitive peoples still living in the interior of Taiwan and south-west China. Chinese penetration into the south began under the Han dynasty (B.C. 207–A.D. 220) and continued slowly until the T'ang dynasty (618–907)—Cantonese people still usually refer to themselves as 'Tong Yan' 唐人—and was fairly complete by the Sung dynasty (960–1280). Pockets of the primitive peoples probably continued to exist in the Hong Kong area but have now become assimilated. The Li Cheng Uk tomb, dating probably from the later Han dynasty (23–220) or from the Six dynasties (220–589), gives evidence of the progress of

The Sung Wong T'oi   *Chung King-pui*
as it was before the Second World War

51

Chinese penetration into the area. Chinese settlement in the New Territories has been continuous from the thirteenth century. The last Sung Emperors fled to Kowloon, and the Sung Wong T'oi, originally a large boulder crowning a small hill and bearing the characters 宋皇台, commemorates their stay here. The Hakka people (stranger or guest families) came into the area about the same time as the Cantonese.

On the island of Hong Kong, the old Chinese name for which was Tai-ki Shan, there was apparently no important settlement. There were, however, small villages which lived by fishing, farming and piracy. The districts of Shek Pai Wan 石排灣 in Aberdeen and Shau Kei Wan were known as the haunts of pirates from the time of the Mongol dynasty in the thirteenth and fourteenth centuries. The modern visitor does not need much imagination to see these bays as pirates' dens.

THE INHABITANTS OF HONG KONG IN 1841

The Chinese inhabitants of Hong Kong even in 1841 were not all from one district of China. The majority were probably Cantonese, known by the foreigners as Punti (Poon Tei 本地) people. These lived, for instance, in the villages at Chek Chue (Stanley 赤柱), and Shek Pai Wan. Other villages, Heung Kong Tsai 香港仔 for instance, were peopled by Hakkas 客家, and there were also some Hoklos 學佬—who provided many of the pirates—while at various points around the coast were the Tankas 蛋家, boat people who did not usually settle on the shore at all.

THE SPEEDY GROWTH OF POPULATION

Once Elliot had occupied the island both foreigners and Chinese came to settle there. The construction work which followed the British occupation meant employment, and the coming of the British meant trade, so the Chinese population soon began to increase. Foreigners, too, soon began to come to Hong Kong for it seemed the safest place to stay when fighting was still continuing between the British and the Chinese forces. The population in May 1841 was probably about 5,650, whereas five months later it was estimated at 15,000.

THE FOREIGN POPULATION

The foreigners fell into five main categories. The first group consisted of the government officials and the army and naval officers; the second group of merchants, members of firms like Jardine, Matheson & Company, Gibb, Livingston & Company, and Dent & Company, and their clerks, often Portuguese from Macao; the third, of the ordinary sailors and soldiers; and the fourth, of the missionaries, English and American Protestants and Italian Roman Catholics. The fifth category, not always distinct from the first three, consisted of the riff-raff which is to be found in any port, the adventurers and ne'er-do-wells.

GEORGE SMITH'S LOW OPINION OF THE PEOPLE

George Smith, who later became the first Bishop of Victoria in 1849, visited the Colony in 1844 to 1846. He was not greatly impressed by the people living in Hong Kong. The foreigners, he said, were hated for their 'moral improprieties and insolent behaviour'. He complained of the frequent scenes in the streets which brought discredit upon the British. Of the Chinese he said, 'the lowest dregs of native society flock to the British settlement in the hope of gain or plunder'. This picture is hardly an attractive one; we can only hope that there were some better elements in the population.

THE DIFFICULTIES AND DANGERS OF THE EARLY YEARS OF THE COLONY

The hazards of life in the new settlement probably led to a certain recklessness in the way of living such as is seen in all new and uncertain settlements. The chief hazards were those of fever and dysentery, which carried off large numbers of people each summer in the early years. Flooding following the summer rains, fires in the dry season, and typhoons, also added considerably to the uncertainty of life and possessions in Hong Kong.

Nevertheless, despite all dangers and difficulties, despite the uncertainty of administration in the first two years of the settlement's existence, 1841–3, despite the undesirable elements in the population, the Colony survived, its population increased, roads were constructed, houses were built, trade grew. This perhaps is a fair commentary on the whole history of the Colony—that despite constant difficulties and dangers it has not only survived but has grown and developed.

CAPTAIN ELLIOT'S ARRANGEMENTS FOR THE ADMINISTRATION OF HONG KONG

From the moment of the occupation of Hong Kong on 26th January 1841, Elliot had to make arrangements for its administration. He could not wait until the final treaty. So on 29th January he proclaimed himself, as Superintendent of Trade, responsible for the government of the island. All Chinese living there or going there were to be governed according to the law of China, 'every description of torture excepted'. All British subjects and foreigners were to be subject to British law.

Two days later Commodore Bremer, the leader of the Naval Forces and commander of the first landing at Possession Point, and Elliot issued a further proclamation. This promised the Chinese inhabitants that they would be protected and that there would be the minimum of interference with them. They would be protected against all enemies and were 'further secured in the free exercise of their religious rites, ceremonies and social customs. . . .' They would be 'governed, pending Her Majesty's further pleasure,

according to the laws, customs and usages of the Chinese
. . . by the Elders of Villages [鄉老], subject to the control
of a British magistrate; and any person having complaint
to prefer of ill-usage or injustice against any Englishman or
foreigner, will quickly make report to the nearest officer, to
the end that full justice may be done'. All Chinese trade was
to be free from payment of customs duties to the British
Government. All heads of villages were to be held responsible
that the commands of the government were observed.

This was a clear declaration of policy, but only of immediate policy; its permanence would have to depend on the
ideas of the government in London.

APPOINTMENT OF OFFICIALS

During the next few months Elliot had to appoint men
to assist him in the task of establishing the new colony.
The names of some of these men are still commemorated
in street names—Johnston Road, named after the first
Deputy Superintendent of Trade; Caine Road, after the first
magistrate, an army officer; Pedder Street, after the first
harbour-master and marine magistrate.

Though Elliot was replaced by Pottinger in August 1841,
following criticism of his policy, his arrangements remained
in force. The growing importance of the new colony was
shown in the spring of 1842, when the headquarters of the
Superintendent of Trade were moved from Macao to Hong
Kong.

A CONSTITUTION IS ESTABLISHED

By the Treaty of Nanking Hong Kong was definitely
ceded to Britain, and so it was necessary to make more
permanent arrangements for the government of the island.
A constitution was therefore established in 1843. First of all
it was laid down that the offices of Superintendent of Trade
and Governor of Hong Kong were to be held by the same

person. As Superintendent of Trade he would be concerned with trade and relations with China, and as Governor he would be responsible for the administration of Hong Kong. This double function might sometimes cause difficulty.

THE GOVERNOR, LEGISLATIVE COUNCIL AND EXECUTIVE COUNCIL

Hong Kong was to be administered by the Governor who, with the advice and consent of the Legislative Council, was to make laws for the peace, order and good government of the Colony. The Legislative Council was to have quite wide powers of discussing and passing laws and the authority to vote taxes, but the Governor was given power to pass laws independently of his Legislative Council should he find it necessary to do so. The Governor, assisted by an Executive Council, was also given the power to carry out the laws, to make grants of land, and to appoint and suspend officials. All these powers were to be used subject to the approval of the Queen, that is the Home Government, who had the final power to approve or disavow anything done by the Governor in Hong Kong.

CENTRALIZATION OF CONTROL

Probably because of the uncertainties of the situation at this time, it was intended to centralize power in the hands of the Governor. No one knew how Hong Kong would develop or what problems would arise. So the Legislative and Executive Councils were deliberately kept small. At first there were only three men in each, in addition to the Governor, and those members were all high officials. The Governor took the lead in passing laws, he enforced the laws, but he always had to report his actions to the Secretary of State in England. He had always to obey the instructions and the general regulations which were issued by the Secretary of State.

As Superintendent of Trade, the Governor was also given authority over British subjects living in China, i.e. in the five treaty ports. In this too the Superintendent was to work through the same Councils and the laws would be largely the same. It would be difficult to enforce such laws in the other ports, but it was felt that most of the British people would observe them. Gradually, however, from 1844 these powers of control by Hong Kong over British subjects in China were reduced; by 1865 none remained.

THE GOVERNMENT OF THE CHINESE IN HONG KONG

It had been agreed that, as originally promised by Elliot, the Chinese living in the Colony would be governed according to their own laws and customs. But how was this to be done? Was there to be a Chinese judge, an official of the Emperor, stationed in Hong Kong? Since Hong Kong had been ceded, how could the Emperor's officers be allowed any powers there?

The law officers of the British Government advised against giving Chinese officials the right to administer Chinese law, for they said that the British Government was now responsible for the good government of the Colony. It could not pass on that responsibility to anyone else, especially as violence and crime were rife. Law and order would suffer still further if responsibility for them was divided between officials of the British Crown and officials of the Chinese Emperor.

It was agreed that Chinese custom and usage should be safeguarded as long as they did not interfere with justice and good order. Where Chinese custom seemed unjust, the matter would be dealt with by a local ordinance. The criminal law enforced would be British, but Chinese punishments were allowed.

An attempt was made to appoint local Chinese elders to be 'tepos' 地保, officers responsible for maintaining the peace, but they were unpaid and this experiment did not last for long.

GOVERNMENT DEPARTMENTS

Another decision which had to be made early concerned the government departments which needed to be set up and the officials who had to be appointed. The chief departments established were those of the Colonial Secretary, the Colonial Treasurer, the Auditor-General, the Surveyor-General in charge of public works, and the Harbour-Master. There were also to be a Chief Justice, a Magistrate, an Attorney-General and a Colonial Chaplain. Pottinger kept in office the men appointed by Elliot and appointed other naval and army men who were on the spot. It was not until the arrival of Sir John Davis as Governor in 1844 that important officers appointed in England began to arrive.

UNOFFICIAL BRITISH REPRESENTATION ON THE LEGISLATIVE COUNCIL

In 1843 Pottinger attempted to set up his Councils, but he could not find suitable men. After the death of J. R. Morrison, an accomplished linguist, in August 1843, he gave up the attempt. Not until the following year were the Councils set up.

As time went on and the number of British residents in the Colony increased, they began to demand that they should be represented on the Councils. They criticized many of the actions of the Government and suggested that the administration would be better if they were represented. The Government would not consider allowing the British residents self-government, for then they would naturally look after their own interests and neglect the interests of the Chinese who formed the vast majority of the population. There was, however, a strong case for some representation, so in 1850 it was agreed that the Governor should nominate two unofficial members to the Legislative Council. The Governor, Sir George Bonham, appointed two of the leading merchants, David Jardine and J. F. Edger, whom the Justices of the Peace had been allowed to choose.

THE ADMINISTRATION AND THE CHINESE

Sir John Bowring, Governor from 1854 to 1859, was in favour of having some elected members of the Legislative Council. He urged that the vote should be given to all who paid a certain minimum amount of land-rent, regardless of race. This plan was not carried out, but in 1855 it was agreed in principle that Chinese could be promoted to responsible positions in the administration. Three years later an ordinance was passed which allowed Chinese to be members of juries and to qualify as lawyers.

When Sir Richard Graves MacDonnell was appointed Governor in 1866, he was instructed that he must not agree to any ordinance 'whereby persons of African or Asiatic birth may be subject to any disabilities or restrictions to which people of European birth or descent are not also subjected'. This was an admirable sentiment but it implied that the idea of leaving the Chinese to be governed by their own officials in accordance with Chinese law was being abandoned. This policy, which had been laid down in the beginning, had proved very difficult to carry out. Now the principle of equality for all before the law was accepted, though it was some time before it was fully implemented in practice.

FURTHER DEVELOPMENT OF THE LEGISLATIVE COUNCIL

Bowring (1854–9) increased the Legislative Council by two more official and one more unofficial members. A change of a different kind was the publication of the proceedings of the Council and the opening of its meetings, from 1858, to the public. This led to greater public interest in what the Council did and to more criticism, particularly among the influential merchants. In the same year the powers of the Legislative Council were increased somewhat when it was permitted to vote the budget. Hitherto it had been able to discuss the budget and to vote on taxes, but not to vote the budget itself.

In 1865, Sir Hercules Robinson (1859–65) fixed the constitution of the Legislative Council more precisely. The five chief officials of the Government were to be ex-officio members, while one other official and three private individuals were to be nominated by the Governor as unofficial members.

A few years later, under Sir Arthur Kennedy (1872–7), the Council was given the power to debate any motion which was properly proposed and seconded. This greatly increased the power of unofficial members to bring up proposals and get them fully discussed. The Council, however, still consisted of European members only.

THE APPOINTMENT OF NON-EUROPEAN MEMBERS

This was changed by Sir John Pope Hennessy (1877–82). Despite opposition from some other officials, he appointed the first Chinese member of the Legislative Council. Ng Choy 伍才,* whom he appointed in 1880, had been born in Singapore and educated at the old Central School (Queen's College) and in England. He was the first Chinese to practise law at the English bar and at the Hong Kong bar. He had already been made an acting magistrate, the first Chinese to hold this post. The year after he had appointed Ng Choy, Sir John nominated a prominent Indian member of the community, E. R. Belilios, to be a member of the Council.

* He left Hong Kong in 1882, entered the service of the Chinese Imperial Government under the name of Wu T'ing-fang 伍廷芳 as legal adviser to Li Hung-chang 李鴻章, and rose to be Chinese Ambassador to the United States in 1899. In the 1911 Revolution, he led the group of republicans who secured the abdication of the Manchus. Subsequently he held the ministries of Justice, Foreign Affairs and Finance under the Republic. He died in 1922.

In 1884, under Sir George Bowen (1883–5), the Legislative Council was reorganized. The official element was increased to six while there were to be five unofficial members. These were to be chosen as follows—the Chamber of Commerce was to elect one, the Justices of the Peace were to elect one, and the Governor was to nominate three, of whom one was to be Chinese. From this time, Chinese membership of the Legislative Council became a permanent feature.

Ng Choy, first Chinese member
of the Legislative Council

LATER DEVELOPMENTS

In 1894, leading members of the British community tried hard to secure control of the Legislative Council. In a petition to the Secretary of State they proposed to introduce elections, but only British subjects, though of any race, could have voted. This would have meant handing over a Chinese majority to the control of a British minority, and the British Government refused. This refusal has been maintained ever since as a general principle.

The main changes since 1894 have been the enlarging and broadening of the Legislative Council to make it more representative of different sections of the community. In 1929 the Council was increased to nine official members in addition to the Governor, and eight unofficials of whom three were to be Chinese. In 1961 it consisted of the Governor, who is President of the Legislative Council, five ex-officio members—the Commander of the British Forces, the Colonial Secretary, the Attorney-General, the Secretary for Chinese Affairs, and the Financial Secretary—four other official members and eight unofficial members nominated by the Governor. These included five Chinese members and one Indian member.

THE EXECUTIVE COUNCIL

The Executive Council, for the first thirty years of its existence, consisted of three members only. Under Kennedy (1872–7) it was increased to five, all officials. In 1884 Bowen added two more members, but these too were officials. Not until 1896 were any unofficial members appointed. In that year two were appointed to represent the general community. Both were influential merchants, J. J. Bell-Irving of Jardine, Matheson & Company, and Paul Chater, an influential merchant born in Calcutta. Lord Ripon, Secretary of State for the Colonies from 1892 to 1895, had suggested that one of the two should be Chinese, but the Governor, Sir William Robinson, had not agreed. Not until 1926 was a Chinese, Sir Shouson Chow, nominated to the Executive Council.

Since then the Chinese representation has been increased and in 1961 the Executive Council had five ex-officio members—the same who serve on the Legislative Council—one nominated official member and six unofficial members who include three Chinese and one Portuguese. This Council, like the Legislative Council, is presided over by the Governor.

THE URBAN COUNCIL

As we shall see in Chapter XI, a Sanitary Board was set up in 1883 to bring about a much-needed improvement in the sanitary conditions in the Colony. This at first consisted of three officials, but in 1885 four unofficial members were added to it. Two years later it was reconstituted so as to consist of four official members and up to six others. Of the six, four were to be appointed by the Governor, two of the four being Chinese and the remaining two were to be elected by ratepayers whose names appeared on the jury lists. This marked the first step towards a local body to deal with municipal affairs and also introduced elections which were not confined to British nationals.

The Sanitary Board survived until 1935 when it was developed into an Urban Council. This consisted of five officials and eight unofficial members. Two of the latter were elected by those on the jury lists and six, of whom three had to be Chinese, were appointed by the Governor. This Council has since been expanded and now has six ex-officio members—the chairman of the Council, who is the Director of Urban Services, and officials concerned with the Health Services, Public Works, Chinese Affairs, Social Welfare and Resettlement—and sixteen ordinary members. Eight of these are appointed by the Governor and eight are elected. The elections have helped to encourage the starting of two incipient political parties, the Reform Club and the Civic Association.

The Urban Council is concerned with sanitary services, public health and resettlement. Its functions are constantly being increased; thus it is the body responsible for the new City Hall.

THE NEW TERRITORIES

We have so far said nothing about the administration of the New Territories. When they were first leased, it was intended that existing village organizations should be used for the administration of the area. This plan did not work very well, since with British officials there the village elders lost authority. Gradually the British officials took more and more control of the administration. In 1910 a new department, the District Office, was created for the administration of the New Territories and by 1913 there were two District Officers, one for the Northern District and one for the Southern District.

The number was later increased to four and in 1960 to five, the work of these District Officers being co-ordinated by a District Commissioner. The District Officers are assisted and advised by Rural Committees, elected by and from village representatives. In addition the leaders of the New Territories have, since 1926, formed what is known as the Heung Yee Kuk 鄉議局, a kind of consultative council. This was reformed in 1959 and given a regular constitution as an advisory body.

THE GROWING SCOPE OF GOVERNMENT

In the early days of the Colony administration was relatively simple. There were only a few departments, already mentioned on page 58. There was also the Registrar-General's Department, set up at the end of 1844, which tried to look after Chinese interests. The Registrar-General was later given the additional title of Protector of the Chinese. The organization of a police force was an immediate necessity, though it was, as we shall see in Chapter VIII, some time before an even moderately efficient force was established.

As time went on more and more departments had to be created. Medical work was at first in the hands of the army and private individuals and the facilities were hopelessly inadequate. In time, however, the government of Hong Kong realized, as the governments of England and other European countries were realizing at the same time, that the State had to play its part in organizing medical services. In the course of the nineteenth century also, a Post Office Department, Education Department, Sanitary Department, and an Import and Export Department were all established. As in the West the tasks of government were becoming gradually more and more complex.

Later still came departments dealing with Commerce and Industry, Agriculture, Forestry and Fishing, the New Territories Administration, and as time went on there came the Urban Council, the Civil Aviation Department and many others. The latest, the Co-operative Development and Fisheries Department, was set up in July 1960. There are now some thirty departments, under the general direction of the Colonial Secretariat, covering all aspects of life in the Colony.

This growing complexity of government is typical of the whole world. The governments of all countries are taking on more and more responsibilities in regulating and controlling and safeguarding the lives and interests of the people. This leads of course to a large growth in the number of government officials. In 1959 the total number of persons employed by the Hong Kong Government was slightly over 45,000, and the salaries for these accounted for about one third of the total government annual expenditure. Many of these employees, Chinese and European, are highly trained officers. One cannot help wondering what Captain Elliot and his handful of helpers would think if they could see their numerous successors today.

Extract from The Times, *15th March 1859, quoted in J. Norton-Kyshe,* The History of the Laws and Courts of Hong Kong, *London, 1898.*

It is now some months since we made passing allusion to the abnormal and not very creditable state of our official arrangements in the little island of Hong Kong. . . The sound of the name (of Hong Kong) in our Parliamentary proceedings . . . is always connected with some fatal pestilence, some doubtful war, or some discreditable internal squabble; so much so that, in popular language, the name of this noisy, bustling, quarrelsome, discontented and insalubrious little island, may not inaptly be used as a euphemous synonym for a place not mentionable to ears polite. We cannot wish that the sea would take it back again to itself, because English lives and English property would be endangered;

but, if these could be withdrawn, we should very willingly resign any benefits which we derive from its possession, to be relieved of the inconveniences which it forces upon us.

Extract from the Government Gazette *of 12th October 1861.*

With a view to supply the Civil Service in Hong Kong with an efficient staff of interpreters it is intended that a certain number of cadetships shall be established, the holders of which are to devote themselves for a certain time after their arrival in the Colony to learning the language.

1st. Three gentlemen will be appointed at once to Cadetships, after a competitive examination by the Civil Service Commissioners, from amongst candidates nominated for this purpose by the Secretary of State.

2nd. Each candidate shall be between the ages of twenty and twenty-three.

3rd. The heads of examination shall be as given below. A knowledge of Chinese is not necessary, but the subjects are selected with the object of giving an advantage to candidates who may be presumed to possess an aptitude for acquiring language.

HEADS OF EXAMINATION

1st Exercises designed to test handwriting and orthography.

2nd The first four rules of arithmetic.

3rd Latin and one other foreign language.

4th English Composition including précis writing.

5th Pure and Mixed Mathematics.

6th History and Geography.

7th Constitutional and International Law.

8th Natural Science.

9th Any two of the following languages not having been taken under number 3. French, Spanish, German, Italian.

Candidates who cannot pass in the first two subjects will be rejected, but those subjects will not tell in competition. Every candidate must undergo a competition in the third and fourth subjects and in any two others he may select.

Extract from an editorial in the China Mail, *11th December 1885.*

' . . . While Sir John Hennessy was malignant and obstructive, Sir George Bowen has been passive and comparatively harmless. . . . It required no talent or capacity to produce something better than the rule of Sir John Pope Hennessy, because it would have been very difficult to have given us anything worse, or even so bad. . . . And had it not been that the consuming yearning for self-glorification of the present ruler had so thoroughly disgusted the community, Sir George Bowen might have left Hong Kong carrying with him the respect of all classes of residents here. Hong Kong is a most unhealthy climate for undisguised humbug; and that is the reason why the representative of Her Majesty does not now possess the regard of her true and loyal subjects.'

Extract from a dispatch from the Secretary of State, Lord Ripon, to the Governor of Hong Kong, Sir William Robinson, 23rd August 1894, in answer to a Petition by the British residents asking for self-government.

Meanwhile it may be deduced . . . that under the existing form of government the population of Hong Kong has in half a century increased (say) twenty fold which is prima facie evidence, as you suggest in your dispatch, that the Colony has been well governed. But a further deduction has also to be made, and that is that under the protection of the British Government Hong Kong has become rather a Chinese than a European community; and the fact that the Chinese have settled in the Island in such large numbers has not only been one main element in its prosperity, but also the most practical and irrefutable evidence that the government, under which a politically timid race such as the Chinese have shown every desire to live, must have at least possessed some measure of strength and justice. . . .

I cordially welcome what is said in the petition as to the skill and energy of the British merchants who have been or still are residents in Hong Kong, and I can testify with pleasure to their public spirit. But the fact remains that the overwhelming mass of the community are Chinese, that they have thriven under a certain form of government and that in any scheme involving a change of government their wishes should be consulted and their interests carefully watched and guarded.

CHAPTER VI

The Trade and Industry of Hong Kong

HOPES FOR TRADE

'Within six months of Hong Kong being declared to have become a permanent Colony, it will be a vast emporium of commerce and wealth.'

This was written by Pottinger early in 1842 and many others in the Far East undoubtedly shared this view. The British had insisted upon the cession of Hong Kong because it would be a useful base from which to safeguard traders and a convenient centre for trade. It would control the British in all treaty ports and would share in the trade with those ports. It would, in particular, dominate the trade with Canton. Instead of British merchants going there to trade, Chinese merchants would come to Hong Kong, and thus the new colony would gradually replace Canton as an important trading centre. It had been prosperous in the closing stages of the war when, despite the hostilities, trade had continued, so there was great disappointment when, following the making of peace, there proved to be less trade than expected.

DISAPPOINTMENT IN THE EARLY YEARS

This disappointment was one reason for a parliamentary inquiry in 1847, but the report of this inquiry did not help to increase trade. There were several causes for this lack of trade. Firstly, there continued to be much direct trade with Canton. British merchants maintained their offices there, for they had of course many contacts in Canton with Chinese merchants and officials, while the Chinese merchants saw no reason for moving to Hong Kong. Secondly, British ships tended to trade directly with the other treaty ports and Hong Kong was not greatly used as a place of transhipment. If the main cargoes were going to Amoy, Foochow, Ningpo or Shanghai, there was no need to unload at Hong Kong. Moreover, the British Government, following the wishes of many people in England, was trying to discourage the opium trade. Though that trade continued and was quite considerable even at Hong Kong, many of the opium ships at first avoided the Colony. The main reason, however, for the disappointment of the merchants was that they had been too optimistic in expecting a tremendous growth of trade. They had exaggerated both the desire of the Chinese to buy foreign goods and their ability to pay for them.

IMPORTANCE OF OPIUM

Yet though there was much disappointment, trade was not unimportant. There are no precise figures for Hong Kong's trade in the nineteenth century, but in 1844 the number of ships which are recorded as having entered the harbour was 538, with a tonnage of 189,257. Three years later the number had increased to 694 ships totalling 229,465 tons, the great majority of these ships coming from the China Coast, Canton and India.

Of the goods imported into China through Hong Kong, opium proved the most important, and in 1845 the Auditor-General said in a report that 80 clippers were engaged in the trade, of which 19 belonged to Jardine, Matheson & Company and 13 to Dent & Company. The annual government report for the same year spoke of opium as the big export and referred to its transhipment at Hong Kong to smaller vessels adapted for the coastal trade. Hong Kong had by now become the headquarters of this valuable trade.

It was estimated that in the period 1845–9 three-quarters of the Indian opium crop passed through the harbour, much of this in the P. & O. ships which were by then operating regularly in the Far East. We mentioned in Chapter II that in the 1838–9 season nearly 40,000 chests of opium were imported into China; in 1854 the P. & O. ships alone imported 46,765 chests, though the trade was still illegal. Curiously enough, after the trade was legalized in 1858 by the Treaty of Tientsin, the annual reports of the Colony no longer show any figures for the trade in opium.

OTHER COMMODITIES SENT INTO CHINA

Salt was also an important article of trade, smuggled to the mainland by fast Chinese craft, thus evading the Chinese government salt monopoly. Later a considerable trade grew up in sugar, but opium remained for a long time the chief commodity passing through Hong Kong to China.

PIRACY

Another factor which hindered the growth of trade with Hong Kong and the treaty ports was the extent of piracy. Larger European vessels were fairly safe from pirates (though not entirely so) but every junk ran the risk of being attacked and captured unless its owners paid protection money. It was difficult to suppress this piracy.

The Chinese authorities took no action to root out piracy and the British were often afraid that action against pirates might involve them in trouble with China. It was difficult to distinguish a pirate vessel from any other and a mistake could well have caused bad relations with the Chinese officials. Moreover, the navy would not, at first, undertake the police action which was necessary to protect ships against pirates (see page 35). As pointed out in Chapter VIII, it was not until the time of MacDonnell (1866–72) that far-reaching measures of control were taken to prevent Hong Kong being used as a centre from which pirates were fitted out and supplied with information.

Yet even if trade did not grow as quickly as had been hoped, the Colony was important in other ways. As an administrative centre it helped to regulate the settlements being formed in the treaty ports. As a naval and military centre it provided for their defence. It also provided the headquarters of important merchant houses which at the beginning preferred to control their agents from the safety of Hong Kong, and which, in the light of later unrest in China, decided that it was wiser to keep their chief centre off the mainland of China. It also developed shipping services and these soon became the mainstay of its economy. Ships which had come from Europe or America or even from India were frequently in need of repair and overhaul by the time they had reached the China Coast. Hong Kong, with its fine natural harbour, was in a good position to provide them with the services they wanted. It also served as a centre where they could replenish their stocks of food and water.

FURTHER GROWTH OF TRADE

As the Chinese population of the Colony grew, so did trade. More and more was imported to feed and provide other needs of the Chinese immigrants; at the same time, through these immigrants more and more goods were sent into China. Gradually Hong Kong became more of a centre for the supply of British goods to China. This was a result of the general growth of European influence in China following the further concessions gained in 1858 and 1860; many Chinese could not avoid seeing Europeans and some came slowly to use certain Western products.

CHINESE EMIGRATION

As the century wore on, the Chinese began to go abroad in increasing numbers. Chinese emigration was really illegal, but it had been going on for centuries and quite large numbers

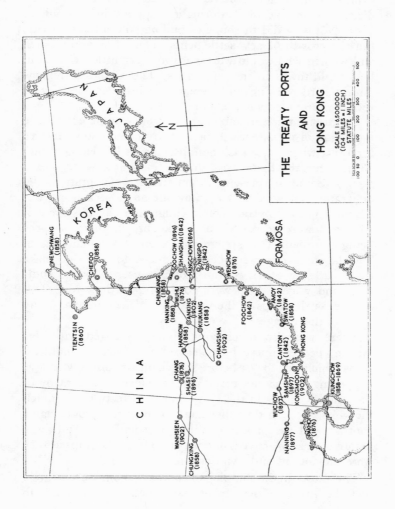

THE TREATY PORTS
AND
HONG KONG

SCALE 1:4,500,000
(104 MILES = 1 INCH)
STATUTE MILES
100 50 0   100   200   300   400   500

CHINA

JAPAN

KOREA

FORMOSA

TIENTSIN (1860)

NEWCHWANG (1858)

CHEFOO (1858)

SOOCHOW (1896)
SHANGHAI (1842)
HANGCHOW (1896)
NINGPO (1842)

CHINKIANG (1858)
NANKING (1858)
WUHU (1876)
ANKING (1902)
KIUKIANG (1858)

WENCHOW (1876)

FOOCHOW (1842)
AMOY (1842)
SWATOW (1858)

HANKOW (1858)
CHANGSHA (1902)

ICHANG (1876)
SHASI (1896)

CANTON (1842)
HONG KONG

WUCHOW (1897)
SAMSHUI (1897)
KONGMOON (1902)

WANHSIEN (1902)

NANNING (1897)

CHUNGKING (1858)

KIUNGCHOW (1858-1869)

of Chinese had gone to the East Indies and Malaya. More recently they had been making their way to the West Indies, to islands in the Indian Ocean, and to Australia. This overseas emigration received a great impetus from the discoveries of gold in California in 1849 and in Australia in 1851. Not only did the hope of finding gold attract settlers, but the growth of new settlements required labourers, men and women who would work hard for very little, who could help build towns in the wilderness. The Chinese, tremendously hard-working and demanding little in the way of rewards, provided such labour.

Figures for this emigration are far from complete but some indication of its extent can be seen from the known figures for 1855, when 14,683 Chinese passengers left Hong Kong, 1857, when the figure was 26,213, and 1859, when it was 10,217. Some of this emigration was free emigration, the emigrants making their own way abroad to seek work, but much of it was contract coolie emigration. By this system, labourers were recruited for work abroad, their passages being provided. This system was often very much abused. The labourers were frequently induced to sign—or make their marks on—their contracts by promises of living conditions and wages which were not kept, and they were often herded on the ships in the worst possible conditions. Many died on the voyages.

There was also much kidnapping associated with this system, poor Chinese being seized and hurried on board ships which put to sea before the victims realized what was happening. It was not many decades since a good many of the English sailors in the Navy had been recruited in much the same way. On the other hand many coolies would sign a contract and accept a money payment and then run away before their ship arrived, or even jump from the ships as they were moving off and swim ashore.

The abuses in the shipping of contract labour were so great that the British Government intervened in an attempt to improve conditions. As a result, in 1858 the Colony prohibited the shipping of such emigrants to foreign countries, though it was still permitted to other British colonies where British officials could see that the ships really did comply with the regulations about accommodation. Hong Kong still remained a great centre for free emigration.

INTERVENTION BY THE BRITISH GOVERNMENT IN HONG KONG AFFAIRS

Intervention by the British Government in this matter aroused a good deal of resentment among merchants in Hong Kong. They felt that they knew the local situation better than the Home Government and that well-meaning intervention on behalf of the Chinese population would lessen the prosperity of the Colony, with which their own prosperity was of course bound up. The British Government, on the other hand, less affected by the immediate question of profits, was able to take a more detached and more humane view. On other occasions also the attitude of the British Government has proved to be more liberal and progressive than that of local British residents who are too concerned with immediate worries to take a longer view. For example, the British Government in 1868 was already urging that public executions should be stopped but this suggestion was successfully resisted by local opinion until 1894. Again, local opinion resisted the stationing of a Chinese consul in Hong Kong which the British Government supported at various times between 1867 and 1885 as a solution of the Hong Kong 'blockade' (see page 41). Such a consul was not in fact stationed in Hong Kong until after the Second World War.

RETURNING MIGRANTS

Hong Kong did not profit only from the emigration of Chinese who embarked on ships in its harbour, but also from the return of many of those who had gone abroad.

These returning migrants not only increased the shipping activity of the Colony but increased its trade in other ways. They frequently brought back not only money which they had saved but also a liking for various Western goods. And so the trade of Hong Kong steadily increased.

THE ESTABLISHMENT OF BANKS IN HONG KONG

The increase of trade led to a need for banks to handle foreign exchange. The first bank in Hong Kong was a branch of the Oriental Bank which was established here in 1845. Before long other banks established in India opened branches in Hong Kong. In 1857 the Chartered Mercantile Bank of India, London and China (now the Mercantile Bank) opened a branch. It was followed two years later by the Chartered Bank of India, Australia and China (now the Chartered Bank). These banks were mainly concerned with currency exchange, but in 1864 leading merchants of Hong Kong established The Hongkong and Shanghai Banking Company (later Corporation). It was intended that this new bank, locally based, should do more to help the trade of the Colony than the existing banks.

In 1866 there was a great economic crisis among foreign firms and banks in the Far East. As a result of this, several banks and companies, including the very important Dent & Company, failed, but The Hongkong and Shanghai Bank survived and soon became the most important bank in China. It became so important that it was later able to take the lead in providing loans to China, Japan and countries in South-East Asia. Thus in 1898 The Hongkong and Shanghai Banking Corporation joined with Jardine, Matheson & Company, to form the British and Chinese Corporation which among other things helped finance the building of various railways including the Shanghai-Nanking Railway, the Shanghai-Hangchow-Ningpo Railway and the Chinese section of the Kowloon-Canton Railway.

Meanwhile the question had arisen as to whether the Colony should establish its own currency. Quite early in the history of the Colony, 1845, it had been declared that English coins, the coins of the East India Company, Spanish and Mexican silver dollars and the Chinese copper cash should all be considered legal tender, and all were given a fixed value in English money. As trade increased, the English and Indian coins gave way to the silver dollars. These were passed, not according to their face value, but 'by weight and touch', a skilled Chinese shroff being able to tell the quality of silver by touch. In 1862, on the advice of the Governor, Sir Hercules Robinson, the British Government agreed that the Colony's accounts should be kept in dollars.

Robinson also proposed that a mint should be opened for minting the Colony's own coins and this was opened by his successor, MacDonnell, in 1866. It proved an expensive failure and was closed two years later.

Towards the end of the century the value of the silver dollar began to fall and this created a good deal of difficulty for traders. There seemed little that the Government could do about this since the currency of Hong Kong was closely linked with that of China owing to the close trade connexion between the two areas. It was not until 1935 that the currency connexion with China was broken and Hong Kong currency was firmly linked to the English pound at the rate of sixteen dollars to the pound.

BANK-NOTES

Meanwhile, since the beginning of the establishment of banks in Hong Kong, some of them had been issuing their own notes. The Oriental Bank had first done this in the 1840s. The Chartered Bank issued its first notes in 1853, followed in 1866 by The Hongkong and Shanghai Bank. Several other banks did the same, but in 1895 an ordinance restricted the issue of bank-notes to three banks only, The Hongkong and Shanghai Bank, the Chartered Bank and the Mercantile Bank.

SHIPPING

Trade depends on means of transport, of carrying goods from one place to another, so the growth of Hong Kong's trade has been linked very closely with the development of shipping lines, which could offer fairly regular voyages between Hong Kong and other parts of the world.

Early in the 1840s the P. & O. line extended its services to the Far East. Before long the ships of this company were carrying a large amount of the trade between Europe and the Far East. Within a few years other companies were established, some dealing with long-distance trade and some with local trade. These were much encouraged by local firms, Jardine, Matheson & Company in particular being concerned with the shipping business. In 1862 a French company, Messageries Maritimes, opened its Hong Kong office, and in 1866 the Pacific Mail Line began its service between San Francisco and Hong Kong. Meanwhile the Canton and Macao Steamboat Company had been formed in 1865 to run daily services between Hong Kong, Macao and Canton. Further lines were developed in the next few years. The Blue Funnel Line and the Glen Line both began sailing to the Far East in the 1860s, while the year 1872 saw the establishment by Butterfield & Swire of the China Navigation Company, to carry goods along the China Coast. Since then many more shipping companies have been formed which link Hong Kong with all the major ports in the world.

SHIPS

The ships which were first seen in Hong Kong harbour were sailing ships, though it was not long before a few steamships—carrying sails too—were seen. Steamships did

78

not become really important in the Far East trade until after the opening of the Suez Canal in 1869.

In the 1840s a new class of ship emerged, the fame of which is not forgotten even now. These ships were the famous 'clippers' which first carried opium from India to Chinese ports and later carried tea from the ports of China to England. The most graceful and the fastest large sailing ships ever built, they raced every year as soon as the winds became favourable from China to London. Each was trying to reach the tea-market in London before the others so as to capture the top prices for tea. The races became world-famous events and the names of some of these clippers were widely known. The most exciting of these races was that of 1866 when three clippers left Foochow on the same tide and, sailing round the Cape of Good Hope, reached London on the same tide 98 days later.

In addition to the clippers which took part in this annual tea-race, there were many others which sailed in and about South-East Asia and which were frequently to be seen in Hong Kong harbour. These clippers lasted into the 1890s, but long before that they were being replaced by steamships. Steamships were able to take advantage of the Suez Canal, and this, together with the building of larger ships with more powerful engines, led to the gradual disappearance of the beautiful sailing ships.

There have been constant improvements in ships since then. Coal has largely given way to oil as the fuel used. Ships have generally become bigger and their design has tended to become more streamlined. They have also become more comfortable, not only for passengers but also for the crews, while modern aids have made them safer than ever before.

SHIP-REPAIRING AND SHIPBUILDING

Soon after its occupation in 1841 the need for ship-repairing yards was felt in Hong Kong. Two typhoons within a week damaged several ships. Almost as soon as the island was officially ceded dockyards were established at East Point and in 1843 the first ship built in Hong Kong was launched from these yards. In 1857 the first dry dock in the Colony was constructed at Aberdeen, and after this there was a rapid expansion in the facilities for repairing and building ships. In 1863 some of the existing companies combined under the Hong Kong & Whampoa Dock Company and by 1880, following further amalgamations, this company controlled nearly all the shipbuilding and ship-repairing industries in Hong Kong.

Early in this century, Butterfield & Swire took the lead in the establishment of the Taikoo Dockyard and Engineering Company. Since then this company and the Hong Kong & Whampoa Dock Company have been the principal commercial dockyards, though there are several smaller companies which are mainly concerned with the small craft in this area. Many ships have been constructed in Hong Kong, including large passenger liners and cargo vessels as well as smaller vessels.

THE COMMERCIAL PROSPERITY OF HONG KONG IN THE LATE NINETEENTH CENTURY

Towards the end of the nineteenth century, Hong Kong saw the beginnings of other industries. With the encouragement of Sir William Robinson (1891–8) various factories were established—e.g. for the making of matches and soap—rattan work was developed, sugar refineries were expanded, while in 1899 the Green Island Cement Company, which had been established in Macao ten years earlier, extended its works to Hong Kong. But such industry was relatively unimportant.

The Colony's prosperity was based on trade. Shipping services, banking and insurance all contributed to the development of that trade. According to the Chinese Imperial Maritime Customs returns, Hong Kong in 1880 handled twenty-one per cent. of the value of China's total export trade and thirty-seven per cent. of her import trade. The Colony was the centre of the opium trade, which amounted in some years to forty-five per cent. of the total value of China's import trade. It was also the centre of the China coasting trade.

In 1866 a total of 3,783 ships of nearly 1,900,000 tons made use of the harbour, excluding junks. By 1898 the figures were over 11,000 ships of more than 13,000,000 tons, and in 1913 the figures were nearly 22,000 ships totalling nearly 23,000,000 tons. The junk trade was also extensive but did not increase in the same spectacular manner, totalling about 25,000 junks a year of between 1,500,000 and 2,000,000 tons. The Hong Kong Chamber of Commerce estimated in 1898 that the total annual value of Hong Kong's trade was £50,000,000.

THE END OF THE OPIUM TRADE

The continuation of the opium trade throughout this period had met with much opposition, in England as in China. In 1874 the Anglo-Oriental Society for the Suppression of the Opium Trade was formed and from then on there were almost continuous attacks on the trade, in Parliament and outside. In 1891 the House of Commons condemned the opium trade but this had no immediate practical result.

In 1906, when the opium trade of Hong Kong was still worth over £5,000,000, the House of Commons again condemned the trade and arranged that exports from India to China should be reduced by one-tenth every year, and so abolished after ten years. In addition the Hong Kong Government was ordered to restrict the use of opium by the closure of the divans. In 1909 the law on opium was revised by local ordinance to give full effect to the decisions of the International Opium Conference, held at Shanghai in February 1909, and to follow the British policy to stop the use of opium. The sale of opium in Hong Kong had long been a monopoly, and the monopolist had the sole right of preparing and selling prepared opium in the Colony and of exporting it. The export of prepared opium from Hong Kong to China and to any other country which forbade its import was declared illegal. Opium divans were to be closed, and their closure, begun in 1907, was completed by February 1910. The trade in opium declined, but the opium monopoly remained in Hong Kong until 1940 and not until then was the use of opium in the Colony forbidden.

SHIPPING AND INDUSTRY AFTER THE FIRST WORLD WAR

The First World War (1914-8) naturally interfered with trade, but after the war Hong Kong again became one of the world's principal ports. In 1919 the shipping figures for Hong Kong were almost up to the 1913 level. The figures continued to increase despite a strike by Chinese workers which began in 1925 and an economic boycott of Hong Kong organized by the Kuomintang in 1926, and despite the world trade slump in the years following 1929. They increased from a little over 26,600,000 tons in 1922 to nearly 42,000,000 in 1931. The peak year for ocean-going shipping using the port was 1935, but then unsettled conditions because of the Sino-Japanese struggle began to interfere with trade.

Industry remained small but was developing. A textile industry had been started at the end of the nineteenth century but had moved to Shanghai in 1914. It was, however, re-introduced and by 1939 employed nearly 6,000 people. During the war, when supplies of European goods were difficult to obtain in the Far East, a number of small factories began making a variety of products such as towels, biscuits, enamel-ware, torches and so on. These factories slowly expanded and by 1939 there were several of them, but the wealth of Hong Kong still lay in its trade and not in its industry. The shipbuilding industry had also expanded and by 1939 employed over 16,000 workers.

After the Second World War had come to an end Hong Kong once again became an important centre of trade. At the same time her industries were quickly re-established and expanded because of the extreme shortage of consumer goods throughout the Far East. Events in China which led to large numbers of refugees entering the Colony helped the expansion of industry, for many of the refugees brought capital with them and many others brought factory experience and technical skill.

The war in Korea and the embargo which was then placed on trade in strategic articles with China (1951) so greatly reduced the volume of Hong Kong's trade that industry had to be developed if economic suffering on a very serious scale was to be avoided. As a result, industry has in recent years become of major importance in the Colony. The industries which already existed have expanded and new light industries have been established.

The textile and garment-making industries have become the most important in the Colony, but a wide range of light metal products is also made, including enamel-ware, aluminium-ware, vacuum flasks, and torches. Much footwear, particularly of rubber, is also made in Hong Kong, while many traditional Chinese goods, previously exported from China to Europe and America, are now produced in Hong Kong.

In 1959 more than 217,000 people were employed in factories, while smaller workshops, mainly engaged in traditional Chinese handicrafts, employed about 150,000 others. Besides these industrial occupations the shipbuilding and ship-repairing industries have further expanded and a ship-breaking industry has grown up. Hong Kong is now the world's largest ship-breaking centre. This industry has led to the growth of a steel-rolling industry which makes use of much of the scrap produced from the ships broken up.

Kam Tin walled village,
dating from the Ming dynasty (1368–1644)

Chiu Tse-nang

AGRICULTURE AND FISHERIES

Little attention was paid to agriculture before the Second World War. The farmers in the New Territories grew their crops and raised their livestock mainly for family subsistence, and when there were surpluses they were marketed in China or Hong Kong. The Government did not bother much about it since Hong Kong's food requirements could always be imported from China. So there was no Fisheries or Agricultural Department.

With the growth of population in the Colony since the end of the war and with the uncertainty regarding future relations with the Communist Government of China, great emphasis has been placed on the development of agriculture. Farmers have been given help and guidance and have profited greatly from the establishment of Co-operatives and Marketing

Organizations. The greatest increase in agricultural production has been in vegetables. Before the Second World War the New Territories produced about one-fifth of the vegetables required in the Colony for a population of about 1,000,000. In 1961, with a population of over 3,000,000, approximately three-fifths of the vegetables required are grown in the Colony.

The fisheries too have expanded greatly since the war, stimulated by government help and by the setting up of a Fish Marketing Organization. The total quantity of fish marketed has increased more than three-fold since 1947.

ECONOMIC CHANGES OF THE PERIOD 1950–61

The Colony of Hong Kong, possessing one of the world's finest harbours, an outpost of the West on the coast of China, is ideally situated to be the centre of trade between China and the West. For a century that trade grew, bringing prosperity to the great merchant houses of Hong Kong. Political developments have limited the use of the Colony as an entrepôt in the past decade, with the unforeseen result that Hong Kong has become an important industrial centre. She now makes for her own use many things which were previously imported, and exports a wide variety of goods to countries in all parts of the world. At the same time she has greatly developed her agriculture and fisheries.

These developments are far from being at an end, for each year sees the growth of new industries. The year 1959, for instance, saw the manufacture of plastic flowers for export to the United States and Europe, while 1960 witnessed the expansion of the aircraft overhaul and repair industry. The changes of the past decade have been so unpredictable that one wonders what surprises the next few years will bring.

Shipping.

Ships entering Hong Kong
(from 1860, numbers entering and clearing)

Year	Number	Tonnage
1844	538	189,257
1850	883	299,009
1860	2,888	1,555,645
1880	5,775	5,078,868
1900	10,940	14,022,167
1920	21,498	21,576,139
1930	28,374	37,909,385
1939	23,881	29,196,466
1950	35,248	26,396,355
1960	38,625	34,886,416

Extract from the Report of the Select Committee of Parliament on Commercial Relations with China, 1847.

From Hong Kong we cannot be said to have derived directly much commercial advantage, nor indeed does it seem to be likely, by its position, to become the seat of an extended commerce. It has no considerable population of its own to feed or clothe, and has no right to expect to draw away the established trade of the populous town and province of Canton, to which it is adjacent. From the only traffic for which it is fitted, that of a depot for the neighbouring coasts, it is in great degree debarred, except in regard to the Five Ports, by treaties which stipulate distinctly for the observation of this restriction.

Extract from the prospectus issued in July 1864, explaining the purpose of the new Hongkong and Shanghai Banking Company.

The local and foreign trade in Hong Kong and at the open ports in China and Japan has increased so rapidly within the last few years that additional banking facilities are felt to be required. The banks now in China, being only branches of the corporations whose headquarters are in England or India and which were formed chiefly with a view to carrying on exchange operations between those countries and China, are scarcely in a position to deal satisfactorily with the local trade which has become so much more extensive and varied than in former years. This deficiency the Hongkong and Shanghai Banking Company will supply and will in fact assume the same position with relation to this Colony as the presidency banks in India or the banks of Australia in their respective localities.

CHAPTER VII

The Growth of Population

THE RECENT INCREASE OF POPULATION

There has been a tremendous increase in the population of Hong Kong since the end of the Second World War in 1945. This growth has led to great difficulties owing to the shortage of accommodation, of jobs, of hospitals, of schools, of public transport, and so on, and has had a great effect on the whole life of the Colony. In more recent years, and particularly as a result of publicity during World Refugee Year, 1959–60, not only the citizens of Hong Kong themselves but people in many other parts of the world have become aware of this growth of population. Yet, though this increase has been greater than any increase in the past, the general problem of growth of population, together with some of the difficulties which that creates, is not a new phenomenon in Hong Kong.

CHARACTERISTICS OF THE POPULATION

Three important points may be made about the population of Hong Kong. First, it has always been a mixed population, made up of men and women of different races and nationalities. Second, it has had a firm and almost continuous growth, though there have been short periods during which it has declined. Third, there has always been a considerable floating section, people who come to Hong Kong for a few years and then leave.

THE MIXTURE OF POPULATION

Most of the people have always been Chinese, but from the beginning there were Europeans and Indians. Even the Chinese were not all of one type, since there were Cantonese,

Hoklos, Hakkas and Tankas even before the arrival of the British, and other Chinese peoples came later. The Europeans too have always been most varied, comprising mainly British people, but also Portuguese, Dutch, Americans and many other nationalities. The *Chinese Repository* of January 1843 lists foreign residents, in some cases rather vaguely, as follows: British 182, American 67, Mohammedan 11, Parsee 46, Swiss 2, French 6, Hindu 3, Danish 2, Spanish 2, Italian 1, Peruvian 1, Dutch 4, Prussian 1, German 1, Hamburg 2. Thus from the start there were many nationalities represented in Hong Kong.

UNEXPECTED GROWTH OF POPULATION

It was not expected at the beginning that there would be a large settled population. Hong Kong, it was thought, would be a trading centre, a place where goods could be stored and transhipped, a market where goods could be bought and sold. It would have a small settled population of merchants and

Aquatint by J. Prendergast

North-east view of Victoria, 1843

administrators, with soldiers and sailors to defend them and their trade, and a number of labourers. Apart from that it would be a centre to which merchants would come, make their sales or purchases and depart. A steady influx of Chinese residents was not expected.

REASONS FOR THE INFLUX

This influx came about for what we might call ordinary reasons and extraordinary reasons. The ordinary reasons were concerned with work and trade. The original occupation of Hong Kong was followed by a good deal of initial construction work. Houses, godowns and roads had to be constructed, and there was a good deal of work in connexion with the navy and with merchant ships, and so work was available. Chinese labourers came to the island, therefore, to earn their living by doing this work. There were also other services which the Chinese could do for the foreigners who had occupied the island, acting as servants, cleaning, washing clothes and cooking, and as commercial employees. As soon as a number of Chinese settled in Hong Kong to work, others came to serve them, opening eating shops and wine shops and tailors' workshops. Chinese merchants came too and found it convenient to live in the Colony or to leave their representatives there, and thus the population grew. Many of the merchants settled in the area of Tai Ping Shan and Bonham Strand, which became the centre of Chinese traders in Hong Kong. In 1887, W. H. Marsh, the Colonial Secretary, reported that the Chinese were flocking to the Colony and 'hundreds sleep in the streets' because the 2·50 dollars a month they could earn in Hong Kong was more than they could get in their village. Though this was much later, it does indicate one of the main reasons for the coming of so many Chinese into the Colony.

The extraordinary reasons were connected with abnormal conditions inside China. In times of difficulty there was a great influx of people. When there was famine, many people would come into Hong Kong seeking work or begging for a living. When there was fighting, people would come seeking refuge. Thus at the time of the T'ai P'ing rebellion large numbers came into the Colony, as can be seen from the population table on page 98. At the time of the Revolution in 1911 there was also a considerable influx, and similarly during the first part of the Sino-Japanese War, until the Japanese captured Hong Kong at the end of 1941, and again during and after the Chinese civil war. In Hong Kong security could be found, until conditions in China improved. Yet always these emergencies brought a number of Chinese who did not afterwards return to their native province but settled in Hong Kong and thus helped to swell the more permanent part of the population.

THE SHIFTING NATURE OF THE POPULATION

Yet though the population grew and though there was a permanent element in it, it was always a shifting population. The numbers increased but the individuals who made up those numbers were constantly changing. Labourers came and worked until they had saved some money, and then returned to their native villages. Merchants came and settled for a few years and then retired to their home towns. For many, Hong Kong was a place where work could be found, where money could be earned, where trade offered the chance of good profits. When the work had been done, the money earned, the profits gained, then the workers and the merchants could return to their homes. This was true not only of the Chinese but even more of the Europeans. Most of them came for a number of years and then, if they had survived the fevers of Hong Kong, returned home. Many Chinese tradesmen and merchants did, however, settle in the Colony permanently, as did some Europeans, particularly the Portuguese. In addition, as time went on there was an increasing number of

Eurasians who regarded Hong Kong as their true home and not just as a temporary place of work.

THE PORTUGUESE

The Portuguese came to Hong Kong largely from Macao. At first they were few in number but gradually more and more moved over, encouraged by various incidents. Thus the murder of Amaral, the Governor of Macao, in 1849, led many Portuguese families to come to Hong Kong for safety, while the destruction wrought in Macao by a typhoon in 1874 resulted in many others moving to the British Colony. But though many came, it was long before most of them became British subjects. Even those born in the Colony did not normally claim to be British until well into the present century.

The Portuguese added a stable element to the community, for whereas the other Europeans tended to come and go, the Portuguese regarded Hong Kong as their home. This permanency, coupled with the fact that many of them grew up with an excellent colloquial knowledge of Cantonese and a great deal of understanding for the Chinese way of life, has enabled the Portuguese to play a valuable part in the development of the Colony.

THE INDIANS

Another section of the community, which helped particularly in the development of trade but later also in social work, was the Indian section. The first Indian merchants to settle in Hong Kong were the Parsees, who because of their links with the East India Company had established godowns and offices in Canton several years before the cession of Hong Kong. From Canton many of them moved to Hong Kong and some of these early families are still established in the Colony. The Indian firm of Abdoolally Ebrahim and Company has lasted from 1842 right down to the present. The first report of the Registrar-General in 1845 numbered 362 Indians in the population. Many of the Indians settled in Hong Kong as permanent inhabitants, thus adding a certain stability to the changing population.

Apart from their trade, the Indians showed enterprise in other ways. Thus it was an Indian, Dorabjee Naorojee, who founded the ferry service between Hong Kong and Kowloon which was later taken over by the present 'Star' Ferry Company. From the beginning, many of the police, and many of the private guards employed by business firms have been Indians.

THE BRITISH

Though there have been some British families with a continuous record of service in Hong Kong, and though there has in many cases been a family tradition of service with certain firms, yet there are comparatively few British families which are established in Hong Kong in the same way as the Portuguese, Indians and Chinese. The British, on the whole, have been temporary members of the community, often spending many years here but tending to centre their lives upon England, to send their children there to be educated and retire there after their years of service in Hong Kong.

THE CHINESE

The Chinese population of Hong Kong was, as we have seen, constantly changing. Yet an increasing number of families did settle here, forming a stable nucleus of the population. Many of these families remained humble trading, labouring or fishing families and we know little of their individual history, but some families achieved wealth and fame and became what might be called the Chinese aristocracy of Hong Kong.

THE GROWTH OF THE POPULATION

Between 1845 and 1898 the population increased from 23,817 to 254,400, and by 1916 this latter figure had more than doubled to 528,010. This rapid increase continued. The next five years saw the addition of another 100,000 and the following four years of yet another 100,000. This growth of population was largely connected with events in China, the revolution of 1911 and subsequent unrest and periods of fighting. These events led large numbers of people, many of them wealthy, to seek safety for themselves and their wealth in Hong Kong. By 1937 the population had passed the million mark. Immigration became even greater in that year and the following years because of the Japanese War against China and the fall of Canton in 1938. About 100,000 refugees entered the Colony in 1937, followed by 500,000 in 1938 and 150,000 in 1939. The estimated population in 1941 was 1,639,000, of whom 1,615,000 were Chinese. The Colony was once again, as at the time of the T'ai P'ing rebellion, a place of refuge for those fearful of the unsettled conditions in their own country or seeking a chance to earn a better living than was possible in those conditions.

THE JAPANESE OCCUPATION AND LATER GROWTH OF POPULATION

During the Japanese occupation of the Colony, 1941–5, the population dwindled and when the Second World War ended in August 1945, it was estimated at less than 600,000. Bad conditions in China and the prospect of better conditions in Hong Kong led to a rapid influx; by the end of 1946 it was estimated that the population had reached the mark of 1,600,000 again. The civil war in China and the establishment of the Chinese People's Republic in 1949 resulted in further emigration to the Colony. This, coupled with an extremely high birth-rate, has caused the population to grow to 3,128,044 according to the census held in 1961.

DIFFICULTIES RESULTING FROM THIS RAPID GROWTH

The growth of population in the past had often meant great overcrowding of available accommodation and added greatly to the difficulties of the police, the medical authorities and all government departments. The enormous increase of the past decade has put a heavier strain upon the Colony than ever before. It is a great tribute to the Government of Hong Kong that so many people could be received and that public services have been able to expand in many directions. It is an even greater tribute to the immigrants, to their patience, their capacity for hard work and endurance, their peaceful nature, qualities which have helped the Colony to develop in a most spectacular fashion.

THE PRINCIPLE OF FREE ACCESS

Why was it that the Government of Hong Kong permitted so many Chinese to enter the Colony at different times? Why did it allow large-scale immigration which was bound to cause great difficulties? The answer lies in nineteenth century liberalism, in an unwillingness to impose restrictions.

The supplementary Treaty of the Bogue, 1843, stated that all Chinese were free to come to Hong Kong for purposes of trade. The British encouraged all to come to Hong Kong, to trade or to live. Not only those who wished to trade could come, but anybody. This liberal attitude became traditional and remained well into the twentieth century, even when the influx was causing tremendous difficulties. At last, in 1950, the Government came to the reluctant conclusion that it could no longer receive large numbers of immigrants for it was not even able to look after those who had already come in. So in that year a quota system was established, preserving a rough balance between those entering and those leaving the Colony across the Chinese border. This was relaxed in February 1956, as it was thought that restrictions might be no longer necessary, but it was re-imposed in September of the same year as many more were coming into the Colony than were leaving it.

The 'problem of people', as Sir Alexander Grantham, Governor from 1947 to 1957, termed it, has turned the attention of the Government increasingly to matters of welfare. In all countries there has been increased emphasis on educational and medical facilities and on social welfare work of all kinds, among the youth, the blind, the crippled, the destitute, and so on. In Hong Kong, developments along these lines would have meant a great effort even if there had been no great increase of population. The greater need called forth extra energy and, despite great difficulties, much has been achieved in the last few years. What has been done, however, has created greater awareness of what needs to be done, and more and more plans are on foot for the expansion of educational, medical and social work.

Extract from a speech by Sir John Pope Hennessy to the Hong Kong Legislative Council, 3rd June 1881, comparing the census returns of 1876 with those of 1881.

There are in this Colony, as you all know, various industries employing Chinese artisans. Carpenters have increased from 2510 to 2923, blacksmiths from 690 to 708, pewter-smiths from 60 to 173, tin-smiths from 88 to 172, and braziers from 488 to 864. Masons show a falling off from 845 to 542. Rice-pounders have increased from 954 to 1083, and in stone-cutters there is a large increase—from 449 to 1439. The number of tailors now in the Colony, who work with sewing machines mostly, amounts to 1847. It is an interesting fact, that for these tailors drill is imported into the Colony from England, they make it up with their sewing machines, and the made clothes are then exported to New Zealand and Australia. In that way Chinese cheap labour, even without leaving the atmosphere of China, is, to a certain extent, successfully competing with Australian and English manufacturers of clothes.

There are certain special occupations of the Chinese which are worth noting, as they indicate their prosperity.

We have the birds' nest sellers, who have increased from 12 to 35, the sharks' fins dealers, from 9 to 15, beancurd sellers from 93 to 107, jadestone dealers from 8 to 18; but cinnamon dealers have fallen from 8 to 7. Sessamum oil dealers appear for the first time, and number 5, and gin seng dealers also appear for the first time and are 4 in number. Joss-paper sellers have increased from 30 to 47, joss-house keepers from 17 to 41 and chair-coolies from 859 to 980.

Extract from the Hong Kong Government Annual Report *for 1958*.

With the British reoccupation, many returned. . . . Many thousands of people, impelled by the chaotic conditions in China at the time, flooded into Hong Kong seeking, in the main, better opportunities and economic security. . . . By the end of 1949 China's new civil war had spread to the Southern provinces. This and the rapid consolidation of the new régime resulted in a fresh influx, greater than Hong Kong had ever known. This time they were mainly political refugees. By May 1950 there was an increase in population of some 700,000 from this cause alone and in addition to the 'economic' increase between the end of the Pacific War and the capture of Canton by the Communists. Restrictions on entry from China were inevitable.

The reader may well ask why this was allowed to happen. A small integrated community with resources appropriate to its size surely has a right to protection against an inundation of strangers. This is an internationally accepted principle. . . . Why was the situation ever allowed to develop into the vast problem that now faces the Government? Was it assumed that up to one million immigrants could be assimilated to an acceptable degree and in reasonable time?

The answer to these questions may fall oddly on modern ears. The immigrants were admitted on humanitarian grounds alone and the problems to which they would give rise if they did not return or emigrate elsewhere were deliberately accepted. . . . Hong Kong accepted the burden which they brought with them in the name of humanity rather than because it had any special standing in the matter other than the accident of contiguity.

Population Table.

Some of these figures are estimates but they are all approximately correct.

Year	Non-Chinese	Chinese	Total
1841	—	5,650	5,650
1851	1,520	31,463	32,983
1861	2,986	116,335	119,321
1871	8,754	115,444	124,198
1881	9,712	150,690	160,402
1891	10,494	214,320	224,814
1901	20,096	280,564	300,660
1911	18,893	445,384	464,277
1921	14,798	610,368	625,166
1931	19,522	859,425	878,947
1941			1,639,000
1951	14,500	2,345,500	2,360,000
1961	47,000	3,081,044	3,128,044

CHAPTER VIII

The Fight Against Crime

CRIMINALS FROM CHINA

One of the first functions of a government is to try to maintain law and order, to prevent crime as far as possible and to attempt to catch those who commit crimes. From the beginning of the British settlement in Hong Kong the maintenance of law and order was a difficult task. The people in the existing villages, living with their families and respecting their village elders, proved no great problem, but new people who soon flocked to the Colony were not all so peaceful.

There were, from the very start, a number of real pirates and robbers who came over from the mainland to steal. For lawless people living on the mainland not too far from Hong Kong, it was a wonderful opportunity to raid shops, houses and godowns. They knew that if they could escape across the narrow straits to the mainland they would be safe from pursuit and punishment.

FREEDOM FROM HOME RESTRAINTS

Apart from these professional gangsters, there were many men who came to the Colony as labourers to earn a living and save some money to take back to their native villages. In Hong Kong, away from their families and from their villages where everybody knew them, these men sometimes got into bad company or decided that they could get money more quickly by robbery than by work. Also, it did not seem so wrong to rob 'foreign devils' as to rob people of their own districts. Moreover gambling became rife, particularly at Yau Ma Tei, and later at Tai Kok Tsui where gambling centres arose in the 1850s.

Not all the Europeans who came to Hong Kong behaved well. Some of the sailors and soldiers were eager to improve their fortune by whatever means they could. They too were far from their homes and often behaved far worse than they would ever have done in their own countries or villages. And of course, many of those who ventured from Europe to places like the Far East, the Australian settlements, the Americas, and so on, were not the most gentle of men.

THE CHINESE ATTITUDE TO LAW

To combat this lawlessness two things were needed: an efficient police force, and the active co-operation of citizens in efforts to prevent crime. Unfortunately it was long before these two conditions were even moderately obtained.

The Chinese attitude to law prevented real co-operation. The Chinese, following their Confucian tradition, did not have much respect for the rigid enforcement of the law. They were much more concerned with individual moral conduct. If any individual behaved badly, he would be dealt with by the family or by the village elders. They would not follow a rigid law, but would punish according to their knowledge of the offender, his position, and the circumstances of the offence. The family and the village had a group responsibility for the good behaviour of their own members and would often share in the punishment given, but they had no responsibility for seeing that others, outside their own narrow community, behaved themselves.

In a village with its native inhabitants this was very good, but it was ineffective in a place where there were many individuals who were far from their families and villages. Unless the whole community co-operated in trying to stop robbery and violence, or unless a strong government efficiently tracked down criminals and punished them, it was difficult to see how order could be preserved and protection given to life and property.

Therefore, the original intention to govern the Chinese inhabitants according to Chinese tradition and usage could not be properly carried out. This was partly because of the absence of traditional community leaders, and partly because the British authorities could not use torture or be so completely ruthless as a Chinese governor might be in times of great lawlessness.

THE SLOW DEVELOPMENT OF A POLICE FORCE

The establishment of an efficient police force was a slow process. Even in England a police force was a new development. The Metropolitan Police Force had been set up in London only in 1829, not without considerable opposition, so it was hardly surprising that many years went by before a really effective force was working in Hong Kong.

THE FIRST POLICE IN HONG KONG

The earliest police, appointed by Elliot at the very beginning of the Colony's history, were all from the Army and proved far from satisfactory. The pay was too low to attract good men. In many cases, men transferred to the police as a means of getting discharged from the Army and then neglected their duties deliberately in order to gain their complete freedom. Sailors waiting for ships were also recruited for the police, but also proved unsatisfactory. It was at times doubtful if the police were more law-abiding than the robbers they were supposed to be fighting.

POLICE OFFICERS SENT FROM ENGLAND

Pottinger, the first Governor, wanted to recruit a police force in England, but the Home Government thought this plan too expensive. Davis, who succeeded him as Governor in 1844, added some Indians to the force, and in 1845 persuaded the Home Government to send out three officers from England. Charles May, a London police officer, was sent out as Superintendent of Police, together with two inspectors. He at once started reorganizing the force, replacing some of the most inefficient Europeans and recruiting more Indians and some Chinese. He also organized water police to patrol the harbour. He tried to improve the efficiency of the force by increasing pay, but for long it remained corrupt and inefficient.

DAVIS' EFFORTS TO CONTROL CHINESE CRIMINALS

In 1844 Davis took two steps to try to limit crime. He appointed Chinese officials who were to help the police, hoping thus to control the Chinese population through their own people, the idea which Elliot had held. This, however, was never successful, partly because these men had no real authority. Had they been paid, they might have made a greater effort.

His other step was to provide for the registration of the population, though in fact this was applied only to the Chinese. He thought this would make it easier to keep an eye on criminal groups among the Chinese.

Yet these measures and the partial reform of the police force did not succeed in making the Colony safe. The merchants still maintained their own private guards, and in the evenings men hesitated before going out alone, for that was to invite attack.

RESTRICTIONS AND PUNISHMENTS

As a result of this lawlessness the Government imposed various restrictions and inflicted harsh punishments. A strict curfew was, for instance, imposed in 1843, forbidding Chinese to be out-of-doors after 9 p.m. without a note from their employers. After dark they had to carry lanterns. This curfew applied to Chinese of all classes and remained in force until 1897.

Punishments such as flogging and the cutting of the queue—a great degradation—were normally added to prison sentences, while the stocks were also used for the punishment of offenders, who were thus displayed to the public. In 1846 the Chinese community protested against the public flogging of fifty-four Chinese, and this protest was echoed in the British Parliament. Discussion of colonial problems in Parliament has frequently helped to bring about improvements, though it has not always been welcomed at the time by colonial administrators.

On the question of harsh punishments, one must remember that reform of the penal system in England had started only a few years before this, and that it was not long since the theft of any article worth more than five shillings could be punished by death. Moreover, owing to the low standard of living of many of the poorer Chinese, a spell in prison was no great hardship, for there they would have better food and accommodation than outside. This is still true now. Since punishment then was thought of solely as a deterrent— to make people frightened to commit crimes—the authorities wished their punishments to act as real deterrents, which the threat of prison did not always do. For this reason also, criminals were hanged in public in the magistracy until 1894.

ABUSE OF THE LAW

Unfortunately the efforts to maintain order were accompanied by several abuses. The police, for instance, earned a bad reputation for being too ready to strike people. Unfortunately too, many Chinese took advantage of the ignorance of their compatriots as to the law and the powers of the police, to blackmail them, pretending that they had broken the law. Some of the police themselves used their power to extort money from Chinese who were ignorant of the law or who had committed offences.

Sir Hercules Robinson, who was Governor from 1859 to 1865, was disgusted by the inefficiency of the police. He felt that the Indians recruited were of a very poor type, physically weak and far from intelligent, while he regarded the Chinese police as being too willing to accept bribes. As for the European police, they were chiefly discharged sailors and soldiers and their average length of service was only three months. Many had to be dismissed for drunkenness. No wonder that the police force did not carry out its duties well!

It was not only the ordinary policemen who were guilty of bad conduct, as the case of D. R. Caldwell shows. Caldwell had come out to the Far East during the Opium War, and being a very competent linguist he became unusually fluent in Chinese. He became interpreter to the Supreme Court and a superintendent of police, in which capacity he led many attacks on pirates. He became Registrar-General and Protector of the Chinese in 1856, but in 1861 was found guilty of associating with a notorious pirate and was dismissed from the government service. Yet he was still almost indispensable because of his expert Cantonese and was frequently called upon to interpret in the Courts and to assist the police with information regarding criminals, and he became a trusted general adviser to the leading members of the Chinese community.

In 1862, in an effort to improve matters, Robinson introduced a Police Ordinance. This reorganized the force, increased the chances of promotion, and raised pay. All men joining the police now had to serve for five years, and if they served for ten they could then retire with a pension. At the same time the policing of the harbour was made somewhat more effective. Yet despite this ordinance the police remained inefficient and the lawlessness continued. MacDonnell, who succeeded Robinson as Governor, found that the police were 'the most ineffective . . . that I ever came in contact with'.

He was indignant about the failure to take any effective action to prevent piracy around Hong Kong. 'Literally nothing is known of the haunts of pirates who frequent Hong Kong, nor of the parties who fit them out,' he said.

MACDONNELL'S POLICY

MacDonnell took energetic measures to improve matters. Strict control of the movement and anchoring of all junks, a system of inspecting them, the strengthening of the water police, and some changes in the law, all helped in the quick reduction of piracy around Hong Kong. On land he tried, unsuccessfully, to end corruption in the police. To improve efficiency he recruited two hundred Sikhs and added twenty Scottish police to the British section. At the same time he approved of more flogging and hard labour and made use of deportation. He gave many convicts the choice between serving their sentence and being expelled from the Colony. Those who chose deportation were branded 'with a small broad arrow on the lobe of the left ear' in order to make their return more difficult.

THE DIFFICULTIES OF MAINTAINING ORDER

This insistence on harsh punishment was because Hong Kong was attracting large numbers of lawless people. The problem of maintaining order was not just a matter of preventing crime among a settled population. It was a matter of trying to dissuade thieves and pirates from coming to a place where crime often did pay and where the risk of being caught was not too great. The very factor of geographical position which made Hong Kong a convenient centre for trade with China, made it also a convenient haunt for thieves. The constant coming and going of people, mainly Chinese but also European, made the task of keeping an eye on suspicious characters a most difficult one. An illustration of this is provided by a great increase in crime in 1876, an increase which Sir Arthur Kennedy, then Governor, thought was due to the reduction of the steamer fare from Canton to ten cents. This enabled large numbers of vagabonds and beggars to make their way to the Colony.

THE REPORT OF 1872

MacDonnell set up a commission of inquiry into the police and this reported in 1872, soon after Kennedy had succeeded him as Governor. This commission recommended an Anglo-Chinese police force with more men and better pay and conditions. Gradually these recommendations were adopted. More and more Chinese were recruited, more men were brought out from Great Britain, and the British officers were encouraged to learn Cantonese by being offered a language allowance.

Chung King-pui

A Hong Kong policeman at the end of the nineteenth century

GRADUAL IMPROVEMENT

It took a long time for the police to become efficient, but from this time on progress was fairly steady. Corruption, however, continued, particularly in connexion with gambling houses. The extent of this is indicated by an upheaval in 1897 when two European police inspectors and one European sergeant were suspended and twenty-two Chinese detectives were banished.

The greatest factor in bringing about an improvement in the efficiency of the police was the introduction of regular training and the constant improvement of that training. The biggest step forward in this respect came as recently as 1948 when the Police Training School was opened near Aberdeen. All male recruits are now given a comprehensive basic training for a period of six months before starting on their duties, and there are many more advanced courses.

Recent years have seen two other important changes in the force. The first was the appointment of Chinese to officer grade, and on 1st December 1954 a Chinese attained gazetted rank for the first time. The appointment of local men to senior posts has helped to encourage co-operation between the Chinese public and the police. A further change which is perhaps also having an effect in creating better relations between public and police was the introduction of women police, the first woman police officer being appointed in December 1949.

THE DISTRICT WATCH FORCE

In addition to the regular and auxiliary police forces there is also a Chinese District Watch Force performing similar duties, but controlled by a Chinese committee under the supervision of the Secretary for Chinese Affairs. It arose out of the general insecurity in the early years of the Colony and the desire of the Chinese to arrange for their own police protection in their own way.

CONTINUANCE OF CHINESE CUSTOM

As we have already seen, it was originally intended that the Chinese in Hong Kong should be governed according to their own laws and customs. This intention had to be abandoned, and the law of Hong Kong for all communities came to be mainly English law. This was supplemented by Hong Kong ordinances passed to suit the needs of the Colony. At the same time Chinese law and customs continued to be recognized in many social respects, as regards marriage for instance, and for a long time the practice of 'mui tsai' 妹仔, a form of child adoption rather like child slavery, was allowed to continue in Hong Kong. This was not finally made illegal until the ordinances of 1928 and 1929, following a resolution passed in the British Parliament in 1922. There are several Chinese customs and social laws which are still followed in Hong Kong though they have been changed both in mainland China and in Taiwan.

OLD PROBLEMS REMAIN

Some of the problems which made the keeping of law and order difficult in the past still remain. To a large extent the Chinese outlook on the law—the desire to keep free of wider responsibilities, to rely for protection on the family, the unwillingness to offer full co-operation to the police—still persists. In the past the coming and going of so many people made the prevention of crime very difficult; the influx of large numbers of people since the end of the Second World War in 1945 has had the same effect. Not all those who have come into the Colony have been law-abiding people. Much of the crime committed in the past has been the result of poverty; the same is true today. Much of the crime in the past was organized by Triad Societies, which have deteriorated from societies for mutual help and protection to societies for extortion and terrorism. Strong action was taken against them in the 1880s; strong action is being taken against them in the 1960s.

THE TREATMENT OF DELINQUENTS

Though many of the problems remain the same, the treatment of delinquents has changed, particularly since the Second World War. In line with developments elsewhere in the world, far more emphasis is placed on remedial work and punishment is no longer thought of solely as a deterrent. Prisoners frequently have an opportunity to learn a trade which might help them earn an honest living when discharged. Juvenile delinquents are frequently cared for in training centres where an attempt is made to fit them for useful lives in society. Much useful work is done by Probation Officers who help to guide many offenders, young offenders in particular, away from crime.

More and more efforts are being made, too, to break up the gangs, the Triad Societies, which so often force people into crime. At the same time increasing efforts are being made to provide remedial treatment for drug addicts—for instance in the open prison at Tai Lam Chung—and to prevent the traffic in drugs which leads to so much misery and so much crime. It is ironic that in this Colony, which was originally ceded in a war connected with the opium trade, one of today's great problems is drug addiction.

The increasing amount of work being done by voluntary societies and by the Government to help the most needy and poverty-stricken people in the Colony is also a powerful factor in the prevention of crime.

The efforts to maintain law and order now are more intensive, better organized, and more enlightened than at any other time in the Colony's history. When one considers the poverty of many of the people, the terribly overcrowded conditions, and the fact that such a large proportion of its inhabitants have no roots in Hong Kong, then one realizes how much success those efforts are achieving.

Extract from the Rev. George Smith (later first Anglican Bishop of Victoria), A Narrative of an Exploratory Visit to each of the Consular Cities of China and to the Islands of Hong Kong and Chusan, *London, 1848.*

The Colony has been for some time also the resort of pirates and thieves, so protected by secret compact as to defy the ordinary regulations of police for detection or prevention. In short, there are but faint prospects at present of any other than either a migratory or a predatory race being attracted to Hong Kong, who, when their hopes of gain or pilfering vanish, without hesitation or difficulty remove elsewhere. At Canton the greatest unwillingness exists in the minds of respectable natives to incur the odium which attaches to any connection with Hong Kong.

A proclamation about child-stealing.

PROCLAMATION

By His Excellency Sir R. G. MacDonnell, Knight, and Companion of the Most Honourable Order of the Bath, Governor and Commander-in-Chief of the Colony of Hong Kong and its Dependencies, and Vice-Admiral of the same.

Whereas the crimes of child-stealing and kidnapping have much increased in this Colony and its dependencies of late, and a new law has provided for the flogging of offenders convicted of these crimes. It is hereby notified that if any person shall give such information, evidence or assistance as that any kidnapper, decoy, or child-stealer be thereby convicted and flogged (or being a woman shall be convicted only) then such person shall receive a reward of $20 from the Colonial Treasury.

By His Excellency's command

J. G. AUSTIN

Colonial Secretary.

GOD SAVE THE QUEEN.

Given at Victoria
Hong Kong, 24th August 1868.

Extract from the Hong Kong Telegraph, *9th March 1898,* *quoted in J.* Norton-Kyshe, History of the Laws and Courts of Hong Kong, *1898.*

One does not need to be fastidious in finding fault with the wretched place in which the Police Magistrate of Hong Kong exercises his functions. We feel pretty confident in saying that there is not a more wretchedly-lighted, ill-designed, and badly ventilated Police Court in all the British Colonies. The room is abominably dirty, the ceilings are festooned with cobwebs. . . . The dock is frequently crowded with prisoners, some in very advanced stages of disease and filthiness, and just about two feet away is the one solitary table that has to do duty for Counsel, press and police officers.

CHAPTER IX

Public Works and Transport

HONG KONG IN 1841

As today's traveller passes through the harbour of Hong Kong and looks towards the north shore of the island, he sees a belt of flat land behind which the hills climb steeply towards, and at certain seasons into, the clouds. This flat land is crowded with buildings. The men who came in 1841 also saw the hills, largely covered with scrub and without the numerous houses which stud them now, but they did not see the belt of flat land which now skirts them. Instead they saw a narrow rim of land, while in some places the hills ran right down into the sea. Not only were there no houses there but the very land on which the buildings now stand was not there either. Reclamation work, building and the construction of roads are now going on faster than ever before, but these activities have been outstanding features of the Colony from the beginning of the British occupation.

QUEEN'S ROAD

Soon after the occupation of Hong Kong on 26th January 1841, the erection of buildings began. These first buildings were made of wood or matshed and were placed quite haphazardly. It therefore became necessary to survey the areas where the settlement was growing up, so as to mark out building sites for public and private buildings and for roads. This was delayed somewhat by the continuation of the war with China and by uncertainty as to the permanence of the occupation. Work was, however, quickly begun on a road which followed an existing track along the shore. By the beginning of 1842 this road, later called Queen's Road, was complete from Cantonment Hill Barracks to Sai Ying Poon.

LAND SALES

In May 1841, arrangements were made for the sale of land, and the first official sales were held in June. Meanwhile some of the Chinese inhabitants had been selling to the merchants land which did not belong to them. To prevent frauds of this kind, the Government took control of all sales of land. All Chinese claiming ownership of land had to prove their ownership. Moreover, Elliot was anxious to prevent speculation in land, for already some merchants, anticipating an influx of merchants from Macao and Canton, were trying to buy up large plots for later resale. The Home Government did not altogether like the arrangements which Elliot made for the sale of land and there was some discontent among land purchasers. If Elliot had made no rules, however, building development would have been quite haphazard and there would have been even more discontent.

GOVERNMENT BUILDINGS

Meanwhile rough matshed buildings had been put up to house the military and the civil officials and to provide them with offices. These buildings were situated at Sai Ying Poon and in the Central District, near what is now the bottom of Garden Road. By the end of 1841 wooden barracks for the troops were being built at Stanley, a prison was ready and other more permanent buildings were being erected in the Central District. In the area between this district and Sai Ying Poon more and more Chinese were building houses and streets were therefore being laid out there.

OUTLYING SETTLEMENTS AND ROADS

In 1842 a settlement was made in the Wong Nei Chong area. This proved an unhealthy district and many of those who moved there died of fever, while others moved away again. In 1845, however, this district, known as Happy Valley, was drained and the settlement there expanded.

By this time troops were also stationed at Aberdeen and Sai Wan, so the roads were being extended. By 1845 Queen's Road reached Happy Valley and a further road continued on to Shau Kei Wan and Sai Wan, a causeway being constructed to carry it across Causeway Bay. Bridle paths had been made leading to Stanley, Pok Fu Lam and Aberdeen. The built-up areas were slowly expanding and the road system was developing.

The early roads were poorly constructed and were often damaged by the summer rains. The wooden bridges were frequently washed away. Gradually the lesson was learnt and roads were metalled and bridges were constructed of stone.

EARLY RECLAMATION

Among the first lots of land to be sold in 1841 were several extending from Queen's Road to the sea. Some of the people who were lucky enough to own these lots soon began to extend their possessions by private reclamation seaward, but this was soon forbidden. Quite early, however, probably in 1842–3, some valuable land was reclaimed, part of it still occupied by the Hong Kong Cricket Club.

A few years later, in 1851, a disastrous fire destroyed many houses in the Chinese part of the city. In the rebuilding of this area a second piece of reclamation was carried out by filling in a creek and building a road there, Bonham Strand. When Sir John Bowring was Governor (1854–9) a reclamation scheme was carried out further east, between Happy Valley and the sea. The area was named Bowrington, a name which is still used for this area. Sir John Bowring also made plans to reclaim a certain amount of land so as to make possible the building of a 'praya', a road running along the whole sea-front of the settlement. Since much of the land along the sea-front was in private hands there was a lot of opposition to this scheme.

This idea had originally been suggested by a far-seeing official, the Land Officer and Surveyor-General, A. T. Gordon, as early as 1843. Now with the growth of trade and the increase of shipping coming into Hong Kong, it was important that there should be public control of the water-front. Owing to the opposition, however, only a part of the plan could be carried out, notably in Bowrington where the land belonged to the Government and was not in private hands.

THE NAVAL BASE HINDERS DEVELOPMENT

Bowring's successor, Sir Hercules Robinson (1859–65) continued with this scheme, but the Navy refused to allow the road to be continued in front of the naval area, and unless the Navy permitted this there could never be a praya right along the water-front.

Some years later, during the governorship of Sir Arthur Kennedy (1872–7), the proposal to continue the praya in front of the naval and military area was renewed. A plan was drawn up for a swing bridge which would enable large ships to pass into the naval yard through the praya which was to be built along the sea-front. The army and naval authorities refused, however, and so the city remained divided into two by the land occupied by the Navy and Army, and linked only by Queen's Road East.

When Des Voeux was Governor (1887–91) negotiations were started with a view to moving the naval base to Kowloon, thus removing the island's 'constriction at the waist', but this idea was given up as too expensive. Des Voeux then proposed building a praya on arches in front of the naval yard, thus allowing ships to enter the dock, but this scheme too was rejected. So the naval base remained an obstacle to the planning of the city until 1960 when the Navy sold part of the site to the Government. The base was then largely dismantled and a road was at last built through it.

Already during the time when Sir George Bonham was Governor (1848–54) it had been suggested that the Peak might be a more healthy residential area than the districts near the sea-shore. When Sir Hercules Robinson was Governor (1859–65) the first attempts were made to use the Peak as a residence. This was further encouraged by Kennedy (1872–7) and roads were then begun there.

SETTLED AREAS BY THE 1870S

By 1870 the various settled areas had become quite extensive. The European civilians were in the central district, Victoria, in Spring Gardens where the coast then ran between Queen's Road East and the present Southorn Playground, in Happy Valley and on the Peak. The military settlements were in the centre—e.g. Battery Path led to Murray Battery, there were barracks on both sides of Garden Road and also where H.M.S. *Tamar*, the naval shore station, now stands—and to the west at Sai Ying Poon, and also out at Stanley, Aberdeen and Sai Wan.

The settlements of the more prosperous Chinese adjoined the European settlement in Victoria, just to the west of it. Farther west lay the poorer district of Tai Ping Shan, and farther west still lay the settlements of Sai Ying Poon near the barracks. These Chinese districts were generally known as bazaars. To the east, between Spring Gardens and Happy Valley, lay the growing suburb of Wanchai.

FURTHER RECLAMATION

While Kennedy was Governor (1872–7) a new area was reclaimed at the edge of Belcher Bay, and the new Chinese settlement of Kennedy Town was established partly on this. A few years later, under Bowen (1883–5) and Des Voeux (1887–91) some of the unhealthy swamp land of Causeway

Bay was reclaimed. The most extensive scheme of reclamation up to that time was proposed in 1887 by Paul Chater, a member of the Legislative Council. This scheme was carried out between 1890 and 1904, a strip of land nearly two miles long and 250 feet wide being reclaimed. The old praya now became Des Voeux Road, some distance from the shore. Twenty years later, in 1922, another large area was reclaimed, this time in Wanchai.

Since the Second World War more land suitable for housing the growing population and for the expansion of industry has been needed, and much of this is being reclaimed from the sea-bed in the harbour. Reclamations in the Central District for the City Hall and the 'Star' Ferry Terminal were completed in 1955, at Causeway Bay for a public park in 1954, and at Kai Tak for a new runway to take the largest planes in 1958. Important reclamation works for the purpose of forming new industrial townships were in progress in 1961 at Kwun Tong, and Tsuen Wan including Kwai Chung. Still more reclamations were being made in the Central District, Chai Wan, Cheung Sha Wan, and Gindrinkers' Bay, and others were planned for Tai Po, Castle Peak Bay, and Sha Tin. The harbour area is thus gradually shrinking.

THE CESSION OF KOWLOON

In 1860 Kowloon was ceded to Britain as far as the present Boundary Street. There was considerable disagreement between the Colonial Government and the Army over the use of this land. The Governor, Sir Hercules Robinson, wanted Kowloon to be used for building and recreation, the south-west portion being developed for commercial purposes with wharves built there. The Army, on the other hand, wanted the whole area for the use of troops. In the end there was a compromise between the two views, Robinson gaining land adjoining deep water for his wharves and commercial

Mee Cheung

Nathan Road at the beginning of the century

Chiu Tse-nang

Nathan Road today

118

development, while the Army could select from the other sites. But the dispute between the Government and the Army lasted until 1904.

SETTLEMENT AND RECLAMATION IN KOWLOON

Very soon after the cession of Kowloon there was some reclamation in the Tsim Sha Tsui district. Wharves were constructed and soon there was considerable settlement in this part. In particular the Portuguese and the Parsees settled in Kowloon in those early days. When Kennedy was Governor (1872–7) regular settlement began also in the Yau Ma Tei area. During this period a wharf was built at Tsim Sha Tsui for ferrying passengers to and from the island, an indication that there was now much traffic passing to and fro. Under Bowen and Des Voeux much malarial swampy land was reclaimed in Yau Ma Tei, to the benefit of both health and settlement.

The main road in Kowloon, Nathan Road, was not built until the twentieth century, during the time when Sir Matthew Nathan was Governor (1904–7), though it followed an earlier, smaller road named Robinson Road. Kowloon was so little built on, that the wide road seemed an unnecessary extravagance and was popularly termed 'Nathan's folly'. Other important roads—e.g. Waterloo Road, Prince Edward Road—are more recent still. In the period after 1922 there was considerable reclamation in and near Kowloon, just as there was in Wanchai on the island. Large areas were reclaimed at Kai Tak, Sham Shui Po and Lai Chi Kok, the first of these areas running across the old boundary of Kowloon and the other two areas lying outside it in the New Territories.

THE NEW TERRITORIES

The New Territories were leased in 1898, as explained in Chapter IV. It was a rural area and there was comparatively little building there until after the Second World War. There was, however, a good deal of road construction, partly for military purposes and partly to enable the farmers to bring their produce more easily to the urban areas. A road was built round the New Territories connecting the chief centres, and this was finally completed in 1920.

TRANSPORT IN HONG KONG

When the earliest roads were being built in Hong Kong people moved about on foot, by sedan chair or on horse-back. Soon horse-drawn carriages were seen. A generation after the cession of the island rickshas were introduced and soon became the chief means of transport.

Residence on the Peak became more practicable and more popular after the opening of the Peak Tramway in 1888. This cable-railway, which went up to Victoria Gap, 1,300 feet above sea-level, made the journey to and from the Peak a much quicker and more comfortable one. There was no motor road to the Peak until 1924 when Stubbs Road was completed.

Meanwhile in 1904 a tram service had begun from Shau Kei Wan to Kennedy Town. It proved very useful and eight years later double-decker trams were introduced. For the first time there was cheap public transport between one end of the island and the other.

Already before the First World War, 1914–8, there were several motor cars in the Colony. The first person in Hong Kong to hold a car licence appears to have been a Dr. Noble, an American dentist and chairman of the South China Morning Post Ltd. He certainly found no difficulty, as the modern driver does, in parking his car in the town.

In the early part of this century one could apparently see horse-drawn buses in Hong Kong, but the introduction of motor bus services came late. Not until 1933 did the China Motor Bus Company and the Kowloon Motor Bus Company begin to operate their buses. These services have expanded greatly, yet the constant growth of population makes ever greater expansion necessary.

LIGHTING AND POWER

Lighting in Hong Kong, both public and private, consisted at first of lanterns which burned peanut oil. An improvement began in 1857 when kerosene lamps were introduced, but these still gave poor light. In 1861 the Hong Kong and China Gas Company began producing gas in Hong Kong. Four years later gas was being used for street lighting, and then gradually gas came to be used more and more, not only for public lighting but also for domestic lighting and cooking. In 1892 the gas company extended its services to Kowloon.

The next big improvement in public lighting came when electricity was introduced. The Hong Kong Electric Company was established in 1889 and by 1891 it was providing a good deal of street lighting and domestic lighting. In 1903 a power station was started in Kowloon by the China Light and Power Company. Only recently, however, has electricity virtually replaced gas as a means of street lighting.

THE KOWLOON-CANTON RAILWAY

In 1898 the British and Chinese Corporation, formed, as we saw in Chapter VI, by The Hongkong and Shanghai Banking Corporation and Jardine, Matheson & Company, gained the concession to build the Kowloon-Canton Railway. The Hong Kong Government later decided that it would itself build the section from Kowloon to the Chinese border. This was begun in 1905 and completed in 1910. The Chinese section from the border to Canton was ready soon after this and through traffic to Canton began in 1911. This railway not only stimulated traffic between the Colony and Canton, but also provided an additional means of transport between Kowloon and the New Territories.

Soon after the cession of Kowloon in 1860, the need for a regular cross-harbour ferry service was felt. In 1870 a Mr. Grant Smith started a ferry service with a steam launch, but this first venture was not a success. Soon afterwards an Indian merchant, Dorabjee Naorojee, started a Kowloon ferry service and this was acquired and continued by the 'Star' Ferry Launch Company in 1898. As more people settled in Kowloon the 'Star' Ferry services expanded, new piers being constructed, more and bigger boats being built, and more frequent crossings made.

In 1901 the suggestion was made by the Harbour-Master, Captain H.M. Rumsey, that a bridge should be built across the harbour, and this project and an alternative scheme for a tunnel have often been discussed since. A firm of consulting engineers reported in 1961 in favour of a bridge.

Though ferries ran regularly between the island and Tsim Sha Tsui before the end of the nineteenth century, there were no regular services between the island and other parts of Kowloon until 1918, though a number of small launches ran a kind of cross-harbour taxi service. In 1918 a Chinese company was given a monopoly to run a service between Victoria and the districts of Mong Kok and Sham Shui Po. Five years later this monopoly was transferred to the Hong Kong and Yaumati Ferry Company, together with the right to run a service to Yau Ma Tei. This company began its services on 1st January 1924, using eleven small vessels.

Even the short journeys across the harbour were not entirely without danger. One evening in February 1925, the Hong Kong and Yaumati Ferry Company boat *Kwong Shun*, crossing between Hong Kong and Sham Shui Po, was seized by pirates off Stonecutters' Island. It was taken towards Macao and the passengers were held for ransom. Though the ferry and all on board were subsequently rescued by the Royal Navy, the company was unwilling to risk another piratical attack, so for the next four years it stationed a ferry as guardship to patrol this ferry route after dark.

Later this company began to run ferries to other districts also, and in 1932, after several years of discussion about the need for a service to carry cars and lorries across the harbour, it started a vehicular ferry. In 1938 it began to operate ferry services to various outlying islands and to other parts of the New Territories. All these services have been gradually expanded and the fleet of ferry boats has grown and improved. The latest service to be introduced by the company, in 1960, is a Round-the-Island trip, which has proved very popular with Hong Kong citizens as well as tourists.

AIR TRAFFIC

The importance of Hong Kong has depended largely on her fine harbour which helped to make her a convenient centre to which ships from Europe and America could come to trade with China. More recently Hong Kong has been linked to other parts of the world by air as well as by sea.

Aeroplanes first landed in the Colony in 1924 when Kai Tak was a small grass area about 400 yards by 300 yards, quite big enough for the small planes of those days. In that year a Flying Club and School were started, but the small airfield was also used by a number of flyers who came to Hong Kong in the course of long-distance pioneer flights. In May of that year Captain Doisy landed in the Colony in the course of a flight from Paris to Tokyo. The next month saw the arrival of some American flyers in the course of a round-the-world flight, of Portuguese flyers coming from Lisbon to Macao, and of a British Squadron Leader who was also attempting a flight round the world.

In 1927 the Government took over Kai Tak, where a private company had been reclaiming land from the sea, and the airfield was extended. The Royal Air Force established itself there while the Hong Kong Harbour Office took responsibility for the civil airfield, the Harbour-Master becoming also the Director of Air Services. Though pioneers continued to land in Hong Kong in the course of long-distance flights, there do not appear to have been any regular air services until, in 1935, experimental flights were made between Hong Kong and Penang to link up there with the Imperial Airways flights from Britain to Australia. Imperial Airways was the predecessor of B.O.A.C. The following year a regular weekly flight was started between Britain and Hong Kong via Penang, the journey taking about nine and a half days. In the same year, 1936, China National Aviation Corporation connected the Colony with the mainland by thrice-weekly flights from Canton to Shanghai via Hong Kong. Meanwhile, in 1935 and 1936, Pan-American Airways were making proving flights across the Pacific and in 1937 came the first trans-Pacific passenger flight to Hong Kong. Hong Kong was thus beginning its development as a major airport as well as a major seaport.

THE POST OFFICE

A Hong Kong Post Office was at work from August 1841, but this was concerned mainly with letters for the soldiers and sailors who were serving with the expeditionary force. In 1843 the Hong Kong Post Office was placed under the control of the British Postmaster-General, who from then until 1860 appointed the Postmasters. In 1860, the Post Office came under the control of the Colonial Government, and two years later the first Hong Kong postage stamps were issued. Hong Kong Post Office joined the Universal Postal Union in 1877, less than two years after this Union had come into existence. This made the sending of mail to Britain and other countries simpler and cheaper.

In 1898 a Post Office was opened in Kowloon, and more recently other branches have been opened in various parts of the Colony.

Until 1869 there was no quick means of communication between Hong Kong and Britain; but in that year the Colony was linked by cable with Shanghai by the Great Northern Telegraph Company, and it became possible to send urgent messages via Shanghai and by overland cable to Britain in hours instead of months. In 1871 a submarine cable was laid which linked Hong Kong with Saigon and thence with Singapore and Britain. This new means of communication created closer links between merchants in Britain and their partners in Hong Kong and between the Government in Britain and that in Hong Kong.

A public telephone system was set up in Hong Kong as early as 1882. There were thirty subscribers in that year but soon the business was closed down. It reopened in 1887, by the end of which year there were fifty subscribers. In 1905 the system was reorganized and more up-to-date equipment was used, with the result that there was a considerable expansion of the telephone service. That expansion has continued ever since, the need for telephones often outstripping the supply.

One other means of communication must be mentioned—radio. Broadcasting began in Hong Kong in 1928. This not only enabled entertainment to be provided for listeners but also kept Hong Kong in closer touch with events in other parts of the world. Although Hong Kong was a British Colony and although there were many Europeans in the Far East and an increasing number of Asians in Europe, yet until the aeroplane and radio came into use China was very remote from Europe. These inventions have made them neighbours.

HONG KONG'S WATER SUPPLY

One of the many problems of Hong Kong today is the shortage of water. This is far from being a new problem for there has been a water shortage ever since the population of the Colony began its rapid growth.

When there were only a few thousand people, the water in the streams and the shallow wells was sufficient. When, however, the population jumped in the 1850s to 50,000, 70,000, and by the end of the decade to over 85,000, the supply of water was far from sufficient. For reasons of health, for sanitation and cleanliness, a larger supply was necessary than could be obtained from wells and hill-side streams.

BOWRING'S OPPOSITION TO GOVERNMENT ACTION

The nineteenth century was a period in which governments greatly increased their activities, but there was always some opposition to the growth of the powers of government. The Executive Council in Hong Kong thought in the middle of the century that the Government should take action to supply water. The Governor, Sir John Bowring (1854–9), thought otherwise and maintained that a private company should be formed for this purpose.

POK FU LAM RESERVOIR

It was not until Sir Hercules Robinson became Governor in 1859 that the Government took any definite action. It then began to construct a reservoir at Pokfulam from which water would be brought to the city. This supply came into use in 1864 and it proved completely inadequate. MacDonnell (1866–72) extended this scheme but the supply was still insufficient; his successor, Kennedy, carried out a further extension, building a large conduit to carry water to the central and western districts of the city.

TAI TAM AND WONG NEI CHONG GAP RESERVOIRS

About this time a plan was prepared for bringing water from Tai Tam to the eastern areas of the city by a tunnel through the hills. On account of the high cost work was not started on this scheme until after the Chadwick Report in 1882 (see page 161), a valuable report on the insanitary condition of Hong Kong. No sooner was the Tai Tam scheme completed in 1889 than a Tai Tam extension scheme became necessary, for population was increasing all the time. Now Aberdeen and Shau Kei Wan as well as the eastern districts were to be served by Tai Tam.

In 1899 yet another reservoir had to be built, this one at Wong Nei Chong Gap. It was followed in 1904 by an additional reservoir at Tai Tam. Less than ten years later the need for more water was so great that the Tai Tam Tuk reservoir was begun, the large dam there being completed in 1917.

KOWLOON'S WATER SUPPLY

Meanwhile Kowloon was beginning to experience a lack of water and between 1902 and 1910 waterworks and a reservoir were constructed there. Just over twenty years later a new scheme, the Shing Mun Valley scheme, had to be started, and in 1935, the year of King George V's twenty-fifth anniversary as king, the Jubilee Reservoir was begun. This scheme was completed in 1937, the dam, 285 feet high, being at that time the highest in the British Empire.

Yet despite all these efforts on the island and the mainland, there was a constant need for more water since population was continuing to grow.

TYPHOON SHELTERS

There was, of course, a lot of construction work with which we have not yet dealt. Some of it, that concerned with education and medicine for instance, will be mentioned in later chapters, but there is much which we cannot touch upon in such a small book. Something should, however, be said of the building of typhoon shelters and of lighthouses.

Hong Kong has been hit by several typhoons in the past 120 years. There were two in 1841, one of which wrecked Captain Elliot's ship. A good deal of damage was done in 1867 when the Colony was twice visited by typhoons, while in 1874 many buildings were destroyed by 'the most destructive typhoon in the history of the Colony'. The twentieth century too has seen a number of typhoons, the most terrible of which was that of 1906. That of 1923 drove sixteen ocean-going ships and river steamers ashore, sinking one ship of 1,700 tons. In 1937 a typhoon caused twenty-eight steamships to be stranded on the shore, sank many junks and sampans, and led to a tidal wave thirty feet high which destroyed villages at Tai Po and Sha Tin and swept away four miles of railway embankment. In June 1960, a typhoon sank many sampans and junks, caused the deaths of over forty people, and made several thousands homeless.

These typhoons and many lesser storms have caused tremendous damage to the small shipping of the Colony. In order to protect the smaller junks and sampans from the danger of storms, therefore, typhoon shelters have been built. Thus a typhoon anchorage was constructed at Causeway Bay in 1883 and one at Mong Kok in 1915.

A further safeguard was the establishment of the Observatory in 1883. The most important function of this has been to give warning of approaching storms, thus making it possible for boats to seek shelter before the full storm was upon them.

LIGHTHOUSES

In an area where storms are not infrequent and where there are numerous islands, lighthouses are a great aid to shipping. There was some discussion in the 1870s about the building of lighthouses, but the best sites lay in Chinese territory and the Chinese officials were not very co-operative in this matter. So lights were erected at Cape D'Aguilar and Green Island in 1875 and at Cape Collinson in 1876. In 1892, by arrangement with the Chinese Government, Gap Light was built about 20 miles south-west from the Colony on a Chinese island called Gap Island. The following year, Waglan Light was erected, also in Chinese territory, but this became British when the New Territories were leased.

POST-WAR CONSTRUCTION

From the beginning of the British occupation in 1841 there has been constant building going on in Hong Kong. Houses, godowns, roads, wharves, reservoirs, have been constantly added to, extended, replaced by bigger and stronger ones. In the years since the end of the Second World War the construction work in the Colony has been going on at a far greater rate than ever before.

The building since the war has spread both outwards and upwards. New areas, at Kwun Tong and North Point for instance, have been built upon, causing the urban areas in Hong Kong, Kowloon and the New Territories to expand, while many of the new buildings extend upwards to many storeys. Most of these new buildings are of reinforced concrete and the speed of construction, once the foundations have been laid, is tremendous. A large proportion of the new building, particularly since the start in 1954 of the big programme of resettlement, has been sponsored by the Government.

In 1961 the Town Planning Board put forward a far-reaching plan for the development of the Central District including new reclamations and the old naval dockyard area. Space for Government offices, public services and small public garden enclosures has been ear-marked, and a feature of the plan is the proposed erection of pedestrian

The Central District in about 1908

The Central District today

areas, nineteen feet above the ground from which vehicles would be barred. This is only a plan, but it shows how the face of Hong Kong is constantly changing.

THE RESETTLEMENT PROGRAMME

This programme arose as a result of the rapid increase in the population of the Colony in the years after the end of the war in 1945. Already before the war there had been insufficient accommodation in Hong Kong, and when the population grew so rapidly afterwards there grew up large squatter areas. In these, people lived in miserable shacks which they had put together out of boards, cardboard, odd sheets of metal—any materials which they could find. These shacks were a health risk and a fire risk and often occupied valuable building sites.

After a disastrous fire on Christmas Day 1953, which destroyed the homes of 50,000 of these squatters, the Government decided to construct large multi-storey blocks to resettle the squatters. In the next six years the Government provided accommodation at very cheap rents for 225,000 squatters, but despite this great effort many squatters remain in their shacks.

THE GROWTH OF TRANSPORT FACILITIES

The extensive building programme, both by the Government and by private companies, has led to the construction of many new roads and the reconstruction of many more old ones. As the volume of traffic increases, with more cars, more lorries and more buses in use, every opportunity has to be taken to improve the roads and in particular to widen many of them.

There have been other improvements in transport facilities also, though these facilities are often criticized as being woefully inadequate. The ferry services have been extended and new piers have been built on each side of the harbour and in several outlying districts such as Tai O and Peng Chau. But the most spectacular construction as regards transport has been the building of the runway at Kai Tak airport. This runway is on a promontory 7,800 feet long and 800 feet wide reclaimed from Kowloon Bay. It is easily able to receive the most modern aircraft.

WATER SUPPLY

Great efforts have also been made to increase the water supplies of the Colony. A new reservoir at Tai Lam Chung in the New Territories was completed in 1957, almost doubling the storage capacity of the Colony's reservoirs, bringing it to 10,500 million gallons. This, however, is far from sufficient to meet the growing domestic and industrial demands for water, and a further reservoir is under construction at Shek Pik on Lantao island. When this is completed in 1964 it will add a further 5,350 million gallons to the storage capacity, but even this will be far from sufficient for the estimated needs of that time. A further plan is now being considered which will turn Plover Cove and Hebe Haven into reservoirs; the former is capable of holding 29,000 million gallons. In addition, an agreement was reached in 1961 with the Chinese People's Republic by which water is obtained from the huge reservoir recently constructed over the border at Shum Chun, a pipe-line having been laid through the New Territories to enable the Colony to make use of this water.

The needs of Hong Kong with its greatly increased and rapidly growing population are tremendous. It will be long before there is no longer work for the construction companies, before there are sufficient houses, public buildings of all types, and roads which can accommodate the increasingly heavy traffic of the Colony.

An editorial from the Hong Kong Daily Press, *24th January 1890.*

The recent rains once again worked up Queen's Road into a quagmire. Some months ago the road was re-metalled on a principle which it was believed would be sufficiently strong to withstand the wear and tear of jinricksha wheels, but it is now as bad as ever. No doubt some sort of a surface could be given to the road which would be able to withstand the cutting action of the narrow wheels, but it seems worth consideration whether it would not be less expensive to accommodate the wheels to the road than to accommodate the road to the wheels. Until jinrickshas were introduced Queen's Road was always fairly clean, even in the wettest weather. As soon, however, as these little vehicles came into use, the state of things was entirely changed and with every shower of rain now the road is worked up into deep mud. An attempt was made to mend matters in the first instance by a regulation that licensed vehicles should have wheels of a certain thickness. Might not another step of a similar kind be taken and all jinrickshas be required to have rubber tyres similar to those of bicycle wheels?

A recent visitor to the Colony remarked that except with regard to business pure and simple we were thirty years behind the times. Perhaps the state of our principal thorough-fare may have contributed to the formation of this opinion, for it must be confessed that for an important town to be without properly laid crossings to its streets indicates to say the least of it a want of attention to those refinements of life that are usually found amongst a flourishing community. If a person wants to cross Queen's Road on a wet day he must either take a chair or be content to wade through the mud. For ladies the road is practically impassable on foot, and visitors at the hotels, if it happens to be wet during their stay, are compelled to confine their shopping to one side of the street.

From the chairman's statement at the first Annual General Meeting of the 'Star' Ferry Company Ltd., 30th May 1899, reported in the Weekly Press, *3rd June 1899.*

The double-ended boats have proved so successful and are appreciated so much by Europeans and Chinese that we propose to replace the two old launches by double-enders as quickly as funds will permit; in fact a third boat would by now have been on the stocks but for a difficulty with regard to the number of passengers the Government will allow these boats to carry. The Government will not license the upper deck because the Ordinance which deals with the subject makes no provision for such a deck or in fact for such boats as these. There is no question whatever of the safety of this deck—it was specially designed to carry passengers and is admittedly a perfectly safe and proper place to carry them. We hope that the Government may take steps to make the necessary addition or amendment to the Ordinance before long.

Report of Captain H. M. Rumsey, Harbour-Master, 1901.

In this large tract of almost unoccupied land (the newly acquired New Territories), we have to hand, at once, the remedy for overcrowding in our City, and if we really mean business when we speak about relieving the pressure in the dwellings in Victoria, we must give all half-measures the go-by in favour of the one full measure of providing housing room whereby the surplus population can be accommodated on the other side of the Harbour. By this means a double purpose will be served, the unhealthy conditions now existing in Victoria will be removed and, at the same time, the New Territory will be opened up and developed, to the advantage of the Public Revenue and the Company generally. But in order to accomplish this, it is absolutely necessary that we should have easy communication with the other side, and by 'easy' I mean something very different from the present ferry service. Communication between Hong Kong and Kowloon should be by means of a bridge across the Harbour. The advantages to be derived by such a means of communication are so obvious that they need hardly be alluded to. The mere thought of the difference between walking over to Kowloon direct, or riding over in a chair or a ricksha, or, better still, in the electric tramcar, compared with the present more or less comfortless passage in moderate weather and no passage in bad weather, should be sufficient to commend the scheme beyond question. Nor is the scheme, in my opinion, anything less than a practical one, for there can be no engineering difficulty, I should say, in building a bridge about one mile long over water averaging in depth about 37 feet and with a maximum of 52 feet at low water. Nor will such a bridge be any practical obstruction or even inconvenience to shipping.

CHAPTER X

Schools in Hong Kong

THE NARROW SCOPE OF GOVERNMENT IN 1841

When Hong Kong was occupied in 1841 it was thought of as a useful base for trade and, in connexion with that, as a convenient naval base. The government set up there would maintain law and order, would build a few roads, would watch the interests and the behaviour of the merchants there and in the treaty ports, but there its responsibility would end. It was not yet accepted, even in England itself, that a government should be responsible for education, sanitation, health, the care of the poor, or the hundred and one other things that a modern government controls.

EDUCATION IN CHINA AND ENGLAND IN THE MID-NINETEENTH CENTURY

In China education was a matter of private arrangement between parents and teachers. Teachers sometimes taught individuals, sometimes they would gather small groups around them, and the pupils paid fees to their tutors. In England there was no education by the State. Children of rich families had tutors or went to private schools, while poorer children either received no education at all or learned a little reading and writing in charity schools, usually paid for by the churches. In doing this the churches were largely concerned with training children so that they would be able to read the Bible. The beginning of State support for education in England came in 1833 when a grant of £20,000 was made to two church education societies for school buildings.

From the beginning of the occupation of Hong Kong, there was some education by Chinese teachers and some by the Christian churches. In 1842, Sir Henry Pottinger gave a grant of land to the Morrison Education Society. The Society had been founded in 1835 in Canton in memory of Robert Morrison, the first Protestant missionary in China. It already helped a school in Macao, and this school was in 1843 moved to Hong Kong. Pottinger not only gave it a site on Morrison Hill but also assisted it with some money. This school, the first to be established by foreigners in Hong Kong, lasted only until 1849 when lack of support forced it to close.

Other schools soon opened. In 1843, the London Missionary Society, through its representative, Dr. James Legge, transferred the existing Anglo-Chinese College at Malacca to Hong Kong. This free school, the forerunner of the present Ying Wa Boys' School, taught Chinese classics, English and the New Testament. A similar school was opened the following year but did not last for long. The Roman Catholics established a school for Chinese children in 1843, in 1845 they opened a school for European boys and soon afterwards one for European girls. An American missionary body also set up a school for Chinese children about this time, but it soon had to close. The Anglican Church, led by the Colonial Chaplain, the Reverend Vincent Stanton, opened a school for English children in 1845 but this did not have a long life. Four years later the Anglican Church opened its first school for Chinese students, St. Paul's College.

GRANTS TO CHINESE SCHOOLS

By this time there were ten Chinese schools of the traditional type, in which the teacher waited for pupils and taught them as they appeared, not in regular classes. In 1845. Charles Gutzlaff, an untiring German preacher and a great linguist who had become Chinese Secretary in the office of Superintendent of Trade, had proposed that the Chinese schools should be given financial assistance. In 1847 it was agreed that grants of ten dollars a month should be made to three of these schools, those at Victoria, Stanley and Aberdeen, which were to be supervised by a committee of three officials. This was the small beginning of the public system of education in Hong Kong. The first annual report of this Education Committee, in 1848, showed that 95 boys were attending these three schools. In 1849 a similar grant was made to a Chinese school at Wong Nei Chong and two years later a school near Aberdeen was also given a grant.

In these schools the traditional Chinese curriculum was followed but some Christian teaching was introduced, at first on a voluntary basis. The committee replaced teachers who were found to be unsatisfactory and by the end of 1850 all the teachers were nominees of the committee and all were Christians. In 1850 the committee recommended that the Anglican bishop, George Smith, should superintend the schools. Two years later the number of clergymen on the committee was increased and the bishop was made chairman. As a result, by 1853 a good deal of the teaching was devoted to the Bible.

CONDITIONS IN GOVERNMENT-AIDED SCHOOLS

When Bowring was Governor (1854–9) the number of schools being aided by the Government rose from five to nineteen. By 1859, 873 boys and 64 girls were attending these schools, though attendance was far from regular. Conditions in the schools were bad, and though an Inspector of Schools was appointed in 1856 he could do little beyond calling attention to the need for improvement. Bowring was anxious for reform but he could do little, partly because of the outbreak of the Second Anglo-Chinese War and partly because of opposition from some of his officials.

His successor, Sir Hercules Robinson, did introduce certain changes, the most important being the merging of the government-aided schools in Victoria into one, the new Central School. This, the ancestor of the present Queen's College, was opened in 1862 with a European, Frederick Stewart, as headmaster. By 1864 it had 140 pupils. Besides being headmaster of the Central School, Stewart had to inspect the outlying schools. He found some of them so bad that their grants were taken away.

FREDERICK STEWART

Stewart did not believe that Christianity should be taught in the Chinese schools, but as long as the Board of Education (which had replaced the old Education Committee in 1860) was under church influence the teaching of the Christian religion in the schools would continue. Bishop Smith, however, retired in 1864 and the following year saw the abolition of the Board of Education. This weakened church influence in government schools and led to less religious teaching in them.

Stewart favoured secular education for two main reasons. In the first place he thought that government policy should not aim at converting the Chinese to Christianity. In the second place he saw that Bible teaching as given in the government schools was useless. In many cases the teachers did not teach the Bible at all but merely took it out when the inspector appeared! He did not, however, interfere with the various church schools in which religious teaching continued as before.

THE GROWTH OF PRIVATE AND MISSION SCHOOLS

Meanwhile the Chinese private schools had been growing in number and so also, though slowly, had been the schools run by missionary bodies, both Protestant and Catholic. The mission schools tended to grow more quickly after the start of the T'ai P'ing rebellion, which led more Chinese of a better class to enter the Colony. The schools grew even more after the end of the Second Anglo-Chinese War, for the Treaty of Tientsin, 1858, permitted missionaries to enter China and so encouraged missionary activity. Nevertheless, in 1865 only a small proportion of the children of school age were attending school, less than 2,000 out of about 14,000.

GOVERNMENT SCHOOLS

In 1866 there were thirteen government schools with 623 pupils, of whom 222 were in the Central School. Stewart, as we have seen, was both headmaster of the Central School and Inspector of Schools. From 1864 he had a European assistant and a second from 1869, but even so it was impossible for him to supervise the schools properly. The standards of teaching were very low and the teachers were not always the most upright of men. In 1862, for instance, the teacher at Tai Tam Tuk was charged with highway robbery. Not long afterwards Stewart found out that the Stanley schoolmaster used to shut his school for several days at a time, opening it only when he heard that the Inspector was on his way!

Stewart knew that many of the schools were bad, but he gradually increased the number of schools. He felt that inefficient schools were better than no schools. By 1872 there were thirty government schools. In half of these the Government paid for the buildings and the whole salary of the teachers, but in the others the Government paid only half the salary of the teachers and left the villagers to pay all the rest of the expenditure. Often they did not pay and the teachers received only half their salary.

In 1872 these thirty government schools had 1,480 pupils; six years later there were 2,101 pupils, though the number of schools remained the same. Only two of these schools were for girls. In most of them only Chinese was taught, but in the Central School English was taught for half the time and, when MacDonnell was Governor (1866–72), some mathematics and science were introduced. The pupils of this school were in great demand and many found good jobs before they had finished the school course. By 1871 the school contained 440 pupils.

GRANT-IN-AID SCHOOLS

Stewart was eager both to improve the low standards in the other government schools and to expand the voluntary schools. He tried to do the former by paying bonuses after the annual inspections. The teacher of a very good school was paid the maximum bonus and the teacher of a very bad school was dismissed. To encourage the voluntary and mission schools, he introduced a grant-in-aid scheme in 1873. By this scheme these schools could be given grants according to the success of their students in an annual examination conducted by the Government. Such schools would, of course, be open to inspection. Six schools were given aid in the first year of the scheme and by 1876 eleven schools were receiving grants.

THE APPOINTMENT OF DR. EITEL

By this time it was too much for any man to act both as headmaster of the large Central School and as Inspector of Schools. So in 1879 the Government in England appointed Dr. E. J. Eitel as Inspector, the Central School having a separate headmaster. Dr. Eitel, a member of the London Missionary Society, was a noted Chinese scholar and he brought to his post great knowledge of the Chinese people.

INCREASED EMPHASIS ON THE TEACHING OF ENGLISH

Meanwhile there had been considerable discussion about the nature of education in the Colony. Hennessy, who was Governor from 1877 to 1882, held that government efforts in education should aim mainly at the teaching of English.

A committee which he appointed to consider the teaching of English in Hong Kong supported him in this. It was decided that the hours of English teaching at the Central School should be increased from four to five daily, while the hours devoted to Chinese should be decreased from four to two and a half. It was also recommended that English should be taught in all government schools, though this proved possible only in a few schools. Eitel, in his report for 1879, also suggested concentration on English, proposing that the Government should set up elementary English schools, leaving the Chinese 'native schools' to themselves.

THE GROWTH OF GRANT SCHOOLS

In the same year an alteration in the conditions on which grants would be made to schools made it possible for the Roman Catholic schools to take advantage of the scheme. Partly as a result of this there was a considerable increase in the number of schools inspected by the Government. The number grew from 47 in 1878 (30 government and 17 grant-in-aid schools) to 80 in 1882 (39 government and 41 grant-in-aid). Most of these schools, 64 out of 80, did not offer any English teaching.

THE FIRST ATTEMPT AT TEACHER-TRAINING

As part of the plan for the teaching of more English, a school for the training of teachers was set up in 1881. Ten students were selected for a three-year course, during which they were to be given an allowance of forty-eight dollars per year. The scheme was not a success and it came to an end in 1883 when only four students remained. Of these only two became teachers.

THE STATUS OF THE CENTRAL SCHOOL

There had been considerable criticism of the Central School, for it was felt that its standards were far too low. One reason for this was overcrowding, and so plans were made for building a new school. Yet despite its low standards, it had a high status. Thus in 1884, at the Annual Speech Day, Bowen, the Governor, announced that twelve pupils had been invited to fill posts in the Chinese Imperial Service. This showed that the development of education in Hong Kong had an importance which went beyond the boundaries of the Colony. From the schools of Hong Kong, China got much help in her efforts to improve her administration and to adopt Western technical methods.

The new school building was opened in 1889, the name being changed to Victoria College. It had 960 pupils. Five years later it became entirely an English school, all teaching being in English except for the teaching of Chinese language and literature. In that same year, 1894, its name was again changed, this time to Queen's College.

BELILIOS SCHOOL

Meanwhile in 1890 a government school for girls had been opened, intended to be equivalent to Victoria College. It had opened with 34 pupils but before the end of the year it had 45. As numbers continued to grow a new building became necessary. This was provided partly through the generosity of a Jewish merchant from India, and Belilios School, named after him, was opened in 1893. It had a Chinese department and an English department and was open to children of all nationalities. By 1898 it had 539 pupils, of whom 233 were English girls.

LOW STANDARDS

Though new schools were being opened, the buildings were generally poor and the educational standards low. A report dated 1887 states that of 204 schools (government, grant and private) in the Colony, only 10 or 12 were in decent buildings. Only very few were aiming at anything higher than elementary education, the chief of these being grant schools—St. Joseph's, St. Paul's, the Diocesan Boys' and Girls' Schools, for instance—and the Central School. The introduction of the Cambridge Local Examination in 1887 helped somewhat in raising the standards of English education, but this took some considerable time.

POOR SCHOOL ATTENDANCE

More than half of the children of the Colony did not attend school at all. In 1898 there were 108 private vernacular schools in which the traditional Chinese education was given without government grant and without government control. Six of these were free schools maintained by the Tung Wah, a charitable organization of which we shall say more in the next chapter, while the others were fee-paying schools. These schools together had nearly 2,500 pupils. The 116 schools which were maintained or assisted by the Government, of which 100 were grant-in-aid schools, had more than 8,000 pupils.

There was in the 1890s discussion about compulsory education for Hong Kong, but this was never introduced. An attendance inspector was appointed in 1893 to try to encourage attendance at school as an alternative to compulsion, but it is impossible to judge the effect of this.

DR. EITEL'S POLICY

Dr. Eitel retired in 1897 after serving as Inspector of Education for eighteen years. He had, during these years, tried to increase the amount of English teaching in schools. He had also encouraged the missionary and other voluntary societies to set up schools, by means of the grant system, while decreasing the number of government schools. Thus the latter shrank from 39 in 1882 to 16 in 1898, while the number of grant-in-aid schools increased from 41 to 100 in the same period. Partly because of this only 1·24 per cent.

of the Colony's revenue was spent on education at the beginning of this century, compared to 5 per cent. spent in 1960–1.

EDUCATIONAL PROBLEMS

Several educational problems came to the fore about this time. British parents demanded separate schools for their children, on the ground that the education of their children together with Chinese children held both back; the needs of the two groups and their background of knowledge were different. At the same time some of the leading Chinese citizens wanted schools where the children of the higher classes would not have to mix with children of the lower classes. Furthermore, Irving, who became Inspector of Schools in 1901, showed himself very keen to improve and expand vernacular education.

COMMITTEE OF INQUIRY INTO EDUCATION

Because of these problems Sir Henry Blake, Governor from 1898 to 1903, set up a committee of inquiry into education. The report of this committee, which was presented in 1902, strongly criticized Chinese vernacular education and also the standard of English teaching. Among its many recommendations, most of which were not accepted, was the establishment of separate schools for European British subjects. The Secretary of State for the Colonies, Joseph Chamberlain, did not approve of racial schools set up only for the British. Yet since it was the wish of the parents, he agreed that a school in Kowloon, which Ho Tung 何東, a prominent local citizen, had presented to the Government for English teaching, should be used for British children. Ho Tung had originally meant his school to be open to all, but he reluctantly agreed to its being used as a British school. This became known as the Central British School, now King George V School.

CHANGES IN THE EDUCATIONAL SYSTEM

Though most of the recommendations of the committee were not accepted, the next few years saw several changes. In 1903 the system of giving grants to schools was changed. Hitherto these grants had been based on the results of examinations conducted by the Inspectors of Schools. Each successful child earned a grant for his school according to the class in which he was studying. This system was now abolished and the grants were based on the Inspector's general report. Increased grants were to be given to schools which employed well-qualified teachers. As a result of this, the number of government and grant schools decreased, but the number of pupils and the cost increased. The schools were larger and their standards improved.

THE BEGINNINGS OF TECHNICAL EDUCATION

Sir Matthew Nathan, who became Governor in 1904, was greatly concerned with education. During his years of office, evening classes in engineering, science and commerce were established, and in 1907 these were organized as the Hong Kong Technical Institute. This Institute also undertook the training of teachers as part of its evening-class work.

THE REGISTRATION OF SCHOOLS

Sir Frederick Lugard, who succeeded Nathan in 1907, was also keenly interested in education. In 1911 he set up a Board of Chinese Vernacular Primary Education, as a result of which vernacular education, so much criticized and opposed by the committee of 1902, was now greatly encouraged. Two years later an important education ordinance extended the power of inspection to all schools. Every school in Hong Kong and Kowloon with ten or more pupils had to register, and the Government could inspect all schools and close inefficient ones. Even the private vernacular schools were now subject to control and the way was clear for an improvement of standards.

Meanwhile there had been an important development in higher education. In 1887 a College of Medicine had been founded by some local doctors assisted by the London Missionary Society. One of the first students was Sun Yat-sen. This College soon ran into financial difficulties and appeals were made to the Government for assistance. In 1901 the Government agreed to give 2,500 dollars per annum, and in 1907 the College was incorporated as the Hong Kong College of Medicine.

In that same year, Lugard suggested that there should be a University of Hong Kong. This would not only help in the training of professional men for the Colony itself but would be of assistance to China also. A committee was set up to consider the matter and finally, after several local citizens had made generous donations, notably Sir Hormusjee Mody who defrayed the cost of the University main building and subscribed handsomely to the Endowment Fund, the foundation stone was laid in 1910. In 1912 the University was opened; it had three faculties—medicine, engineering and arts—both the College of Medicine and the Technical Institute being incorporated into this University. Four years later the first degrees were granted.

The University was at first for men only, but in 1921 women students were admitted. The University gradually expanded and this required more money, so since 1920 the Government has given assistance. A new faculty was added in 1939 when the Science Faculty was opened. When the University first opened in 1912 it had 72 students; at the beginning of the 1961–2 academic year it had about 1,550. By 1966 it is expected that the numbers will reach 1,800.

CHANGES IN EDUCATION IN 1921

While the University had been developing, there had been changes in the organization of school education also. In 1921 a Board of Education was set up. This consisted of officials of the Education Department and representatives of the community. This Board had advisory powers only, but its existence stressed the importance of education to the community as a whole and emphasized the responsibility of the community to see that proper schools were provided.

In the same year a change was made in the system of giving grants. The old system was abandoned except for a few schools, while other schools were given subsidies subject to inspection reports. A further development extended compulsory registration of schools and thus inspection to the New Territories.

An important development began in 1922 when the beginning of school medical inspections showed that some responsibility was being taken for the health of school children; from 1926 a schools medical officer was appointed.

EXPANSION OF EDUCATION

There was a large degree of illiteracy in the Colony but the numbers of children attending the schools were increasing. In 1923 there were 23,000 children in the urban schools and nearly 5,000 in the rural schools. Schools for European children were also provided, those over the age of nine going to the Central British School in Kowloon. Before long more facilities were provided for the training of teachers. Teachers were still being trained at the Technical Institute, part of which continued to exist separately though another part of it had been attached to the University. From 1919 to the Second World War a four-year course—a degree and teacher's course—was offered at the University. Moreover Normal classes were being conducted by the Education Department, students combining actual teaching with part-time study. In 1925, the training of teachers for rural schools was begun at Tai Po. In 1939 the Northcote Training College was opened, so that at last a real course of training could be given to teachers for both Anglo-Chinese and vernacular schools.

Secondary education slowly expanded also. In 1926 a second government school on the lines of Queen's College was opened and named King's College. Soon afterwards Clementi Middle School was opened, a government secondary school which gave instruction in the medium of Chinese. In 1932 a Junior Technical School was opened, followed five years later by the Government Trade School, the parent of the present Technical College.

EDUCATION SINCE THE END OF THE SECOND WORLD WAR

The end of the Second World War brought a new spirit to Hong Kong, a new concern about matters like social welfare and education. Ideas which had been developing actively for several decades, ideas about equality, about education for all, about medical attention for all, were taken more seriously. But the problems were very great, and when the civil war in China began and more and more people flocked into Hong Kong they became greater.

After the end of the war, schools were reopened and the numbers of children at school rapidly increased. In 1945 there were just over 4,000 at school; in 1946 there were 65,000. By the next year the number had increased to 100,000 but there were still 60,000 or more without education. Parents were more interested than ever before in getting their children into school. Consequently, not only the number of government, grant-in-aid and subsidized schools increased, but also the number of private schools. By 1954 over 250,000 children were at school but still the places available were far from being sufficient.

THE SEVEN-YEAR PRIMARY SCHOOL PLAN

In that year a more energetic attack than ever before was made on this problem. A seven-year plan was made which aimed at creating enough places in primary schools so that all children could attend school by 1961. That plan proceeded steadily and the proposed number of places were ready by 1961, but the number was still insufficient. In any case there will still be need for constant expansion because of the growth of population. Moreover, a comparable effort will have to be made to increase the number of secondary schools. Though this number has increased somewhat, it has not increased in anything like the same degree as the number of primary schools. In 1961 the total number of children in schools inspected by the Education Department exceeded 600,000.

TEACHER-TRAINING

There has been a great improvement in the training of teachers and a great expansion in the numbers being trained. Northcote Training College has expanded and is shortly to move to new and larger premises. It secured a partner when Grantham Training College was started in 1951, its building being opened in 1952. The University started a course for the Diploma of Education in 1952, and thus contributed to the expansion of schools in Hong Kong. The total enrolment for full-time teacher-training courses in 1959–60 was 732, while enrolment for in-service training courses for unqualified teachers was 1,260.

OTHER POST-WAR DEVELOPMENTS IN EDUCATION

A further change in the education system was the opening of the European schools to all races. The children admitted have to be sufficiently fluent in English to be able to benefit from the instruction, for the standard of English is considerably higher than in most Anglo-Chinese schools. There is, however, no distinction of race.

Events in China, in addition to bringing more people into Hong Kong and creating a demand for more schools, also led to certain colleges moving from the mainland to the Colony. Thus a number of post-secondary colleges were set up. Largely financed by aid from the United States of America they provide a post-secondary education, largely in the Chinese language and on the American pattern. Efforts are now being made to develop these colleges into a Chinese University.

In the schools the curriculum has been changing, as indeed it has been changing in many other parts of the world. More English is being taught than ever before, even in the primary schools. In the secondary schools, there is more and more emphasis on science. There has also been a greater emphasis on technical education and, as Hong Kong becomes more and more industrialized, that branch of education requires more and more attention. This greater emphasis on technical education has been marked by the renaming of the Government Trade School as the Technical College in 1947, and the building of well-equipped premises for it in 1958. Meanwhile, in 1952, a technical school for girls, the Ho Tung Technical School, was opened.

In many other directions, for example in technical education, the teaching of English, and in evening classes, there has been tremendous expansion. In addition to more formal classes in many subjects, there has been a promising development in the opening of Adult Education and Recreation Centres where informal activities of many kinds are developed.

The educational problems of Hong Kong are very great and much thought, imagination, hard work and money need to be expended on them. Yet certainly more energy and thought are being devoted to them than ever before. There is a sense of urgency now which was not evident before the last war, let alone the last century.

Extracts from the report of Frederick Stewart, the Inspector of Government Schools, 15th February 1869.

I arrived in the Colony early in 1862. During the previous two years the schools had been under no regular supervision. Only occasional visits were paid to them by members of the

Board of Education. On 10th March, 1862, the Central school was open for the first time. I found myself on that day among a crowd of nearly three hundred boys, who could not speak English to me and to whom I could not speak Chinese. The Chinese assistant-masters were present, but they had almost forgotten any English they ever knew, and I could scarcely make myself intelligible to them.

The first striking incident that occurred during the year was the trial of the school-master, and three of the villagers, of Tai Tam Tuk for highway robbery. This did not tend in those early days to make my monthly visits to the schools at all pleasant excursions. I was prepared to meet ordinary highway robbers, who were then by no means uncommon, on the Stanley and Shau Ki Wan roads, but scarcely so to come into collision with a Government school-master and his allies at some convenient turn in the road.

Extract from a report on Victoria College (later Queen's College) by the headmaster, Dr. G. H. Bateson Wright, 10th January 1890.

Chinese boys, as a rule, are very intelligent, docile and painstaking. That they are intelligent is established by the large number of boys, that in the short period of five or six years have advanced from the alphabet to a knowledge of English sufficient to do a creditable paper on a play of Shakespeare. Their docility arouses the admiration of every new master from England. Painstakingness is a national characteristic sometimes provoking to the more impetuous European. It might be thought that with these admirable traits the work of teaching in this College would be an easy task and the results should be even higher than they are. There would be grounds for this supposition, if there were not serious compensating drawbacks such as the following. Stolidity and absence of facial expression render it next to impossible for a teacher to gather how much of what he says is understood by the class; he has not the satisfaction of seeing perplexed ignorance dissolve into triumphant knowledge, for difficulties do not pucker the brow, nor does success kindle the eye of the Chinese student.

CHAPTER XI

Sickness, Sanitation and Social Welfare

SICKNESS AND SANITATION

A spokesman of the World Health Organization was reported in the press on 7th April 1960, as saying with regard to Hong Kong:

'Since 1956 there have been fewer *cases* of malaria each year than there were *deaths* from malaria ten years earlier. There have been only six deaths due to malaria during the past four years. In the urban areas, which contain five-sixths of the total population of Hong Kong, no cases of malaria have originated during the past two years.'

EARLY UNHEALTHINESS OF HONG KONG

Hong Kong was first occupied in January 1841. During the first summer the Colony suffered an epidemic of fever, and the deaths were sufficiently numerous to require the setting out of a cemetery. The following year saw a similar epidemic. In 1843 the sickness was even worse. One regiment, stationed at West Point, lost one hundred men between June and the middle of August. An attempt to settle in Wong Nei Chong had to be abandoned for a time, as we saw in Chapter IX, because the area proved so unhealthy. Though health gradually improved there were still many bad years, the chief sufferers being the European troops while the Chinese were the least affected. Thus in 1848, deaths among the European troops rose to 204·3 per thousand, while among the Chinese they amounted to only 11·4. The following year the mortality figures dropped sharply, but in 1850 the European troops had a mortality rate of 239·4 per thousand.

Queen's Road Central in 1867

Queen's Road today

Eleven years later the death rate among Europeans and Americans was 60·8 per thousand, while in 1871 it was down to 30·3.

MALARIA

This fever which killed so many people must have included several diseases, but the most widespread was malaria, the disease which has now almost disappeared from Hong Kong. It was not until 1897 that Sir Ronald Ross showed that malaria was spread by a species of mosquito, and not until 1902 that a deliberate attempt was made to destroy the breeding grounds of mosquitoes.

DRAINAGE SCHEMES

Nevertheless it was realized from the beginning that there was a connexion between sanitation and health and between swamps and ill-health. A Committee of Public Health was therefore set up in 1843 to make a code of sanitary rules for the protection of health. Unfortunately this committee did little. At the same time, however, some drainage work was begun, and in 1846 Wong Nei Chong valley was drained, making that area far less unhealthy than before. The question of sanitation was one which was to be discussed often in the future, but it was long before the problems were energetically tackled.

THE INSANITARY CONDITION OF HONG KONG

In 1854, Dr. J. Carroll Dempster became the Colonial Surgeon and he severely criticized the sanitary system of the Colony. He spoke indignantly of the filth, the nuisances and the stagnant pools of Hong Kong. He pointed out the need for more drains, sewerage, pavements and scavenging. In the following years he continued to complain about these things, growing more and more indignant because very little was done, and more and more impatient with the reply to his recommendations that the matter was 'under consideration'.

In addition to malaria and other 'fevers', smallpox had appeared in the Colony and in 1857 there was an outbreak of cholera. It became even more essential that improvements in sanitation should be carried out.

INSPECTOR OF NUISANCES

Bowring (1854–9) had some new drains constructed and some bins made for garbage, but these measures were quite ineffective. Scavenging, which was carried out by convicts under police supervision, was not done at all efficiently. An attempt to improve conditions by a Building and Nuisances Ordinance in 1856 failed owing to the opposition of the property owners, both Chinese and European. The latter wanted no interference with their property or how they built; the former resented any interference by the Government at all. A sign of improvement came in 1859 when an Inspector of Nuisances was appointed, but it was a long time before the Inspector could really achieve anything.

The problem of sanitation was largely bound up with the water supply. While there was no adequate water supply, it was difficult to keep buildings and drains clean. Until 1864 there was no supply apart from wells and streams, and even after 1864 and right down to the present the water supply has never been adequate.

THE SANITARY COMMITTEE, 1862

In 1859 a new Colonial Surgeon, Dr. I. Murray, arrived in Hong Kong. He proved just as critical of the sanitary arrangements—or rather the lack of them—as Dr. Dempster had been. A Sanitary Committee was appointed in 1862, largely because of the need to prevent the further spread of cholera. Its report in 1863 said that the drainage system of the Colony needed complete reorganization, but no important action was taken.

It is surprising that in these circumstances there were no great epidemics. This must be attributed largely to a great resistance to disease in the Chinese who formed the bulk of the population. We have already seen that when, in 1848, deaths among European troops were over 200 per 1000, the death rate among the Chinese was only 11·4. The following year the rates were much lower—for European troops 79 per 1000, for European civilians 50·6, and for Chinese only 6·1. Since the Chinese population changed so often, owing to the numbers who came from the mainland and those who returned to their native villages, one cannot rely too much on these figures. They do, however, indicate the hardy nature of the Chinese.

CONTINUED MEDICAL CRITICISM OF SANITATION

Dr. Murray continued to call attention to the insanitary condition of Hong Kong year after year. In 1870 he pointed out that, despite his complaints and the report of the Sanitary Commission, the drains remained 'a source of disease and death'. He retired in 1872 but his successor, Dr. Phineas Ayres, Colonial Surgeon from 1873 until 1897, was no less critical. He condemned the insanitary nature of the houses, their overcrowding, the keeping of pigs in the already congested rooms, the lack of drains and sewers. A report by the Surgeon-General of the army medical department, who visited Hong Kong in 1880, also condemned these conditions very strongly. As a result of this, the Secretary of State for the Colonies decided to make a full-scale inquiry into the sanitary condition of Hong Kong. Osbert Chadwick, an engineer, was appointed to carry out this task.

EARLY HOSPITALS

The epidemics of fever meant that permanent hospitals had to be established very early in the history of the Colony. In 1844 a small hospital for seamen was established at West

Point by contributions from the leading merchant firms. About the same time plans were made to replace the existing matsheds in which sick soldiers stayed, by a more permanent military hospital. At this period, too, the Medical Missionary Society of Canton established a hospital near Morrison Hill for the treatment of the Chinese.

THE APPOINTMENT OF A COLONIAL SURGEON

There was so much sickness in Hong Kong that Pottinger wanted to appoint a Colonial Surgeon. He did appoint a Dr. Dill temporarily, but the British Government refused to agree to a permanent appointment, because it felt that private and missionary doctors and hospitals could be employed to look after the police and the lower grades of government servants.

In 1847, however, it was decided to appoint a Colonial Surgeon and Dr. Morrison was appointed. He soon found that he had to set up a hospital in which he could put sick government officials, for it was impossible for him to visit them all in their homes, especially during the summer season when sickness was at its height. Though the Government in Britain had refused to set up a civil government hospital, Bonham (1848–54) took a house in 1848 to serve as a civil hospital. In view of this definite action which, Bonham maintained, was essential owing to the 'present unhealthy state of the Colony', the British Government agreed to a hospital.

THE DUTIES OF THE COLONIAL SURGEON

Though Dr. Morrison and his successor, Dr. Dempster, had this civil hospital under their care, this did not serve the general public except in cases of accident. These Colonial Surgeons were responsible for the treatment of the lower ranks of government servants, police and convicts, but had no responsibility for the general health of the people of

Hong Kong. The idea of a government taking responsibility for public health was not accepted in any country, so it was not surprising that the powers of the Colonial Surgeon were so limited. As we have already seen, however, the holders of this post constantly attacked the sanitary system of the Colony, urging the Government to take action to improve matters and trying hard to improve medical arrangements.

A NEW CIVIL HOSPITAL

When Dr. Murray came to Hong Kong as Colonial Surgeon in 1859, he was able to take over a new and larger civil hospital, and it became necessary to appoint another doctor as medical superintendent of the hospital. The hospital was soon further enlarged and for the first time destitute Chinese were admitted as patients. Most Chinese were suspicious of Western medicine and preferred to trust in their own doctors and herbalists, as indeed many still do. The majority of patients, therefore, were European. The first medical superintendent did not prove particularly conscientious and was soon dismissed. It was found that he used to lock his door at night so as to prevent the Chinese attendant from waking him to deal with accidents or other emergencies!

THE TUNG WAH 東華 HOSPITAL

In the 1850s and 1860s a Chinese temple, the 'I Ts'z' 義祠, situated at Tai Ping Shan, had come to be used as a hospital for dying Chinese of the poorer classes. It was also used as a place where the dead could be stored in coffins until they could be sent back to the native villages. Conditions in this temple were very bad. Criticism by the Government and in the Press led to an improvement, so that some medical treatment and better attention were given to the desperately sick people who were sent there. Conditions were still not good, however, for this temple did not have the space to look after the sick properly.

Encouraged by assistance from the Government, the richer Chinese now subscribed towards the building of a hospital, and in 1870 an ordinance set up the Tung Wah Hospital for destitute and dying Chinese. The hospital was opened in 1872 in Po Yan Street, the directors being prominent members of the Chinese community.

THE GOVERNMENT HOSPITAL

Meanwhile the government hospital which had been opened in 1859 was proving much too small, even though it was used mainly for Europeans. When Dr. Ayres became Colonial Surgeon in 1873 he at once pressed for a new hospital. The matter was made more urgent by the typhoon of 1874 which destroyed the existing hospital. A temporary home was then found for it, but this was destroyed by fire in 1878. The government hospital was then established in a new school building at Sai Ying Poon and in another small hospital.

THE CHADWICK REPORT

In 1881, as we have already seen, Osbert Chadwick was appointed to inquire into the sanitary condition of Hong Kong. He made a thorough investigation, trying hard to find out the views of the Chinese who formed the majority of the population. In 1882 he produced his report. This marked an important point in the history of the health service of Hong Kong.

Chadwick was very critical of conditions in the Colony. He criticized the inadequate water supply and the inadequate plans to increase it; he criticized the houses; he said that the town should be completely re-drained; he demanded more thorough scavenging by an organized sanitary staff. He suggested that the district watchmen should be given extra pay and made responsible for enforcing cleanliness in their districts, and thus the co-operation of the Chinese would be secured. He demanded more public baths, and new and cleaner markets.

THE SANITARY BOARD

When Chadwick had made his report, the Government had to decide what reforms should be carried out. The British Government saw from the report how bad conditions were and insisted on a Sanitary Inspector being appointed immediately. Marsh, who was heading the Government at this time between the departure of Hennessy in 1882 and the arrival of Bowen in 1883, set up a Sanitary Board. This Board consisted of the Surveyor-General, the Registrar-General and the Colonial Surgeon, the officials most concerned with plans for sanitary reform. Sir George Bowen added two more members to this Board, the Sanitary Inspector and the Captain Superintendent of Police. A strong Board such as this should have been able to carry out wide-spread reforms. An ordinance was introduced by the Governor to give the Board powers to deal with insanitary houses and to prevent the spread of disease. Unfortunately this met with great opposition and was withdrawn, so hardly anything was done.

THE PUBLIC HEALTH ORDINANCE, 1887

In 1886 Marsh, who was again administering the Government for a short while, added four unofficial members to the Board. He hoped that this might lessen public opposition to the proposal to give more powers to the Board. This body then proposed an ordinance to set up a partly elected municipal Board of Health which should have powers to enforce better standards of housing, ventilation, drainage, and so on. Property owners, particularly the Chinese owners, strongly opposed the ordinance, fearing that better standards would mean less economical use of building space and thus smaller profits for the property owners. The general public also feared it, thinking that it might lead to higher rents, so the Public Health Ordinance which was passed in 1887 was far weaker than that which had been proposed, owing to the opposition of property owners who thus hindered improvements in sanitation and health. It must be remembered, however, that there was no strong tradition in East or West of governments having great powers in matters of public health. So it was not unnatural, though regrettable, that people opposed the growth of the power of the Government, government 'interference' as it is called by those who dislike it. Every fresh extension of government interest always meets with opposition, which in later years often seems to have been short-sighted and selfish. In this particular instance, men wished to build as they liked, without the Government imposing minimum standards on them.

The ordinance of 1887 set up a Sanitary Board of four official members and not more than six other members. Four of these (two of them Chinese) were to be appointed by the Governor. The other two were to be elected by rate-payers whose names were on the jury lists. This, as noted in Chapter V, marked the first introduction to Hong Kong of elections to a government body.

FAILURE OF THE SANITARY BOARD

Although the powers of this ordinance were so limited, there was still much opposition to it. Owing to this opposition, the Sanitary Board did very little to deal with the overcrowding and insanitary conditions, even though a committee of inquiry emphasized in its report in 1890 the serious nature of the overcrowding.

REFORMS BASED ON THE CHADWICK REPORT

In public works, however, much was done to carry out the recommendations of the Chadwick Report. New main drains and sewers were built, the Tai Tam Water Scheme was begun, unhealthy swamps at Causeway Bay and Yau Ma Tei were reclaimed, scavenging was reorganized, more inspectors were appointed to supervise cleanliness, and a new central market was opened for the better handling of food.

WESTERN MEDICAL TREATMENT FOR CHINESE

Meanwhile there was a growing concern for free hospital treatment by Western medicine for the Chinese. This was partly due to a desire to bring the benefits of Western medicine to the Chinese, but partly to the realization that an epidemic, if ever it started, would know no racial boundaries and would endanger all people in Hong Kong.

Dr. Young of the London Missionary Society began a free medical service for Chinese at the Society's chapel in Tai Ping Shan before 1882. In 1886 the foundation stone of the Alice Memorial Hospital was laid in Hollywood Road. This hospital was built by Dr. Ho Kai 何啟, who had qualified in England both as a barrister and as a doctor, as a memorial to his English wife, Alice, who had died in 1884. The work of this hospital expanded and, as there was no room for an extension in Hollywood Road, a new hospital, called the Nethersole Hospital, was built in Bonham Road in 1893. In 1904 the Alice Memorial Maternity Hospital, the first maternity hospital in Hong Kong, was built from subscriptions by Ho Kai and other Chinese and two years later the Ho Miu Ling Hospital was built, bearing the maiden name of Ho Kai's sister. These four hospitals, all managed by the London Missionary Society, have merged into the Alice Ho Miu Ling Nethersole Hospital.

THE COLLEGE OF MEDICINE

When the Alice Memorial Hospital was founded, it was announced that 'it is proposed to attach a school of European medicine and surgery for the instruction of Chinese students'.

This college, the Hong Kong College of Medicine for Chinese, was set up in 1887 with the aid of the London Missionary Society and local doctors. It was a private college, the doctors giving their services as teachers, and was centred in the Alice Memorial Hospital where the students lived and were taught. Later the Nethersole Hospital also co-operated. From 1901 the Government gave a grant to the College, as we have seen in Chapter X, and when the University was established this college formed part of it.

VICTORIA HOSPITAL

To commemorate the Diamond Jubilee of Queen Victoria's reign in 1897, the Victoria Hospital for women and children was built by public subscription and handed over to the Government. This hospital provided treatment for private patients, Chinese and European, and for government employees. Before many years had passed a government maternity hospital, the Tsan Yuk Hospital, was built.

NURSING

Though there were hospitals and doctors there was still no proper nursing service. Those who worked in hospitals received little pay and were often poorly educated and dishonest. In 1890, however, five nurses belonging to a French religious order were appointed, and in the same year English nurses began to arrive. They were put on the permanent staff of the Government in 1894. The following year the recruitment of Chinese nurses was suggested and this started soon afterwards. In 1897 it was proposed that a nurses' training centre should be built, but unfortunately this proposal was dropped in favour of the Victoria Hospital, so those who became nurses received no proper training. In 1902, however, some nurses came out from England to help with a programme to train private nurses.

Western medicine was still not trusted by the majority of Chinese. Yet surprisingly they did not object to the introduction of compulsory vaccination of children against smallpox. This was started in 1888, following a serious epidemic of smallpox in the previous year.

THE PLAGUE

In 1894 the Colony was attacked by plague. This was common on the China Coast but it was the first time there had been any serious epidemic of it in Hong Kong. In May alone several hundreds died. There was no knowledge of what caused plague, but the Sanitary Board took energetic action to see that the infected districts were cleaned and disinfected, that the sick were removed, that dirty and insanitary houses were cleaned, and that buildings declared unfit for habitation were evacuated. There were house-to-house visits in the infected areas to see that the sick were taken to hospital, and several emergency hospitals were set up.

The Chinese complained bitterly against these things. They were deeply prejudiced against Western medicine and they disliked the interference which these measures meant. The removal of those sick with the plague, the collection of the bodies of all those who died from it, the condemning of many buildings and the dislodgement of those living in them, all aroused great ill-feeling. The Tung Wah Hospital wanted to be made responsible for treating all Chinese who caught the plague, but the Governor would not allow this as the Tung Wah could not deal with the large number of patients involved.

The unpopular but necessary measures which were being carried out led to an increase in anti-Western feeling. This showed itself in the rumours which led large numbers of people to leave the Colony, rumours such as that which accused Western doctors of using the eyes of newly born children in the treatment of the plague.

The plague did not come in that year alone but recurred in several subsequent years; 1896 saw more than a thousand deaths from plague and 1898 was also a bad year. To try to remove the conditions which helped the plague to spread, fresh laws were passed to limit overcrowding and to make the drainage of houses by the Public Works Department compulsory.

THE APPOINTMENT OF A MEDICAL OFFICER OF HEALTH

The epidemics led to much criticism of the Sanitary Board and as a result a Medical Officer of Health was now appointed and attached to the Sanitary Board. The Colonial Surgeon had been mainly concerned with the treatment of the lower grades of government officials, though he had, through his position on the Sanitary Board, come to have a wider influence on health in the Colony. Dr. Ayres retired in 1897 after being Colonial Surgeon for twenty-four years. Dr. Atkinson was appointed Principal Civil Medical Officer and he soon began reorganizing the Medical Department. It was during his period, in 1902, that all ranks of government servants became entitled to free medical attention.

THE INQUIRY INTO THE TUNG WAH HOSPITAL

The plague epidemics led to criticism of the Tung Wah Hospital as well as of the Sanitary Board. Western medicine proved unable to defeat the plague, but Chinese medicine had been no more successful. Moreover the Tung Wah committee had opposed those measures which tried to limit the spread of infection—notably the house-to-house visits to make certain that all infected persons were taken to hospital. The Tung Wah Hospital had been allowed to admit some plague victims, under government medical supervision. As a result of this limited supervision, government medical officers in 1896 said that the Tung Wah Hospital should be replaced by a government hospital for paupers. A commission of inquiry into the Tung Wah was therefore held.

The report of this commission recognized that the Tung Wah had done good work for the Chinese sick and poor, but proposed that it should now be supervised by the Medical Department. It also proposed that a Chinese resident surgeon, trained in Western medicine, should be appointed to give Western medical treatment to those patients who wanted it. The Tung Wah directors were opposed to all interference by the Government, but had to agree to the appointment of Dr. Chung Yik-sun, trained in the Hong Kong Medical College. Dr. Chung was paid by the Government. The directors also had to agree to daily inspections carried out by a European medical officer. There proved to be less prejudice against Western medicine than had been expected and by the end of the century about half the patients were choosing Western treatment.

THE PLAGUE CONTINUES

Despite all efforts, however, the plague continued to kill many people year after year. Professor Kitasato, a Japanese, working with a fellow-countryman, Dr. Aoyama, was the first to discover that the plague bacillus was carried by rats. He made this discovery in Hong Kong in 1894, but it was some time before this connexion between plague and rats was generally accepted. A commission of inquiry into the connexion was dissolved in 1900 because the Medical Officer of Health thought it was an absurd suggestion! However, Sir Henry Blake, Governor from 1898 to 1903, started a great campaign against rats. He offered a reward of two cents per rat which brought in 43,000 rats in 1900, but many of these had probably been specially imported from the mainland in order to earn the reward!

Blake also tried disinfecting the worst areas, but still the plague continued. He appointed more inspectors to try to maintain public cleanliness, and tried to limit overcrowding by laws which limited the extent to which rooms could be sub-divided into cubicles.

CRITICISM OF THE SANITARY BOARD

There was a strong feeling that the Sanitary Board and the Government which controlled it had done too little to improve sanitary conditions. In 1901 the Chamber of Commerce presented a petition, supported by a thousand signatures, asking for a commission of inquiry. Consequently, two specialists were sent out from Britain in 1902, Professor W. J. Simpson of the London Hospital for Tropical Diseases, to deal with plague and malaria, and Osbert Chadwick, once again to deal with sanitation, drains and housing.

THE RECOMMENDATIONS OF SIMPSON AND CHADWICK

In 1897 Ross had discovered that malaria was carried by the anopheles mosquito. Simpson therefore said that nullahs should be kept disinfected, swamps should be drained and the breeding places of mosquitoes should be treated regularly. With regard to plague he said that all houses should be made rat-proof. Though war on rats continued, this particular measure was not enforced.

Chadwick urged further efforts to increase the water supply. To make housing more sanitary, he advised the Government to take back land on which the accommodation was insanitary and then to rebuild. A number of buildings were demolished and the Tai Ping Shan area, for instance, was largely rebuilt, but there was great reluctance to demolish any houses which still provided accommodation, however insanitary they might be. As population continued to increase, particularly with the coming of refugees in 1911 and 1912, the Government became even more reluctant to

Happy Valley and the race-course in about 1856,
with Morrison Hill in the background

Happy Valley and the race-course today,
with Morrison Hill levelled to the ground

demolish any buildings. Moreover, the Government was unwilling to face the opposition from property owners which such action would bring about. Even sanitary regulations for new buildings were often disregarded, the sanitary inspectors themselves accepting bribes from the building contractors. Private gain was put before the good of the community.

A DECLINE IN EPIDEMICS

Improvements did take place, however, and the number of cases of plague and malaria decreased. After 1924 there was virtually no plague in the Colony, while deaths from malaria gradually declined though they still remained numerous until after the war. The changing and increasing population of Hong Kong, however, brought constant difficulties. For one thing, overcrowding was never eased, despite a series of Building Ordinances which tried to improve matters. For another, the Colony could not be kept free from infection, especially when there was an influx of refugees. Thus there were serious outbreaks of smallpox and cholera in 1937 and 1938.

EXPANSION OF MEDICAL FACILITIES

Medical facilities slowly increased. In 1926 the Kowloon Hospital was opened, while in 1937 the large Queen Mary Hospital, replacing the old government civil hospital, was built. During the same period other hospitals were opened or expanded. All the time Western medicine was increasing in popularity and more and more Chinese came to the government hospitals and clinics for treatment.

THE URBAN COUNCIL

In 1935 the Sanitary Board blossomed into the Urban Council. The Board had been much criticized throughout its existence, and though it had done a good deal to improve sanitation it could have done far more. It was constantly hampered by lack of power to enforce better sanitary conditions.

The Urban Council, of which we have already said something in Chapter V, was given powers to frame and carry out bye-laws, subject to the consent of the Legislative Council. It had charge of all sanitary services in the urban area, and as the years passed more duties and powers were given to it.

THE SECOND WORLD WAR

The slow but steady expansion of medical facilities was interrupted by the war. Even before the war broke out the influx of refugees from China as a result of Japanese attacks had brought great health problems to the Colony. These problems got worse when Japan and Britain were at war, 1941–5. Tuberculosis spread rapidly while many of the people of Hong Kong suffered from diseases such as beriberi as a result of the great lack of food.

POST-WAR IMPROVEMENTS

When the war ended in 1945, there was a new sense of urgency about tackling problems of health, just as there was about educational problems. The tempo of change, once the administration had been set up again, became much faster than before. Yet fast though it was, it still could not bring about all the necessary improvements quickly enough.

The doctors were assisted by the great advances made in medical knowledge but handicapped by the rapidly increasing population. Overcrowding became worse, and though plague had disappeared and malaria had diminished, tuberculosis remained very widespread. With expanding staff, new buildings, new methods of treatment, however, the medical authorities have helped to maintain a surprisingly high level of health among the people.

In addition to the expanding government services, there have been established many organizations which, with public and private help, are helping to improve medical facilities. The Anti-T.B. Association, for instance, has done much valuable work, while the work carried out among lepers on the island of Hei Ling Chau has met with extraordinary success.

THE GROWTH OF GOVERNMENT RESPONSIBILITY FOR HEALTH

For the first forty years of the Colony's history the Government, while to some extent looking after the health of its own officials, showed little active concern about the general health of the Colony. After Chadwick's report in 1882 there was greater activity in sanitation, and that same decade saw the introduction of compulsory vaccination for children. From then on Western medicine was gradually made more available to the ordinary Chinese of Hong Kong. At first the missionary groups did most, but especially since the First World War, the Government has shown an increasing interest in this direction. For the richer section of the population these facilities were always available from private doctors, but for the poorer people Western medicine could be obtained only from missionary and government doctors.

CHINESE MEDICINE

All the time there were Chinese herbalists and doctors who practised Chinese medicine. At first all the Chinese of Hong Kong preferred traditional Chinese treatment, but gradually suspicion of Western treatment diminished. More and more Chinese began to turn to Western-trained doctors, though there are still many who go to such doctors only when their own Chinese medicine fails to cure them. Often the Chinese medicine does harm, particularly in the treatment of eye diseases, but some Chinese methods have proved of value and more is now being learnt about these traditional methods.

The greater energy of the Government nowadays in providing hospitals and clinics for the treatment of sickness and accident and the great advances in medicine are helping to diminish disease despite the overcrowding of the Colony. At the beginning of the chapter we saw that malaria had almost entirely disappeared from Hong Kong. Plague has disappeared and so has smallpox. The death-rate has diminished and in 1959, at 7·1 per thousand, was the lowest on record. An indication of the increased government facilities for medical treatment and of the willingness of people to take advantage of these facilities is shown by the attendances at government clinics and dispensaries. These attendances increased by 118 per cent. between 1953 and 1959, from 2,340,682 to 5,107,644.

SOCIAL WELFARE

It is only fairly recently that governments have done much social welfare work, work to help the poor and distressed. In England there was comparatively little such work carried out by the Government before the First World War; in Hong Kong there was even less. In both England and Hong Kong, however, there was some social work done by voluntary societies, though this was more widespread in England than in Hong Kong. Most voluntary effort in Hong Kong went into education and medicine and there was little other social work.

REASONS FOR THE LACK OF SOCIAL WORK

There were two main reasons for this lack of social welfare work in the Colony. Firstly, there was the strong family sense of the Chinese. It was the duty of the family to look after its own members who were in trouble, even if the relationship was very distant. This meant that, on the other hand, there was no sense of responsibility for anyone outside the family. Secondly, there was the variable nature of the population.

This meant that when people were in distress they could go back to their native villages and families for help; it also meant that any schemes for giving help to the poor and distressed might have the effect of attracting large numbers of such people from China.

THE PO LEUNG KUK 保良局

The first Chinese charitable body to be set up was the Tung Wah, which was mainly concerned with caring for the sick but also helped the destitute. The Tung Wah Hospital, as we have already mentioned on page 161, was opened in 1872.

Another important charitable organization, the Po Leung Kuk, was formed in 1880 and officially recognized by the Government in 1882. The object of this was to protect women and children against kidnapping, for large numbers of women and girls were being sold for service in Hong Kong and overseas. This practice was an abuse of the accepted Chinese custom of 'mui tsai', the purchase of children for adoption and especially for use as domestic servants. There was much disagreement about this among the British officials. Some wished to stamp out the practice entirely while others felt that the Chinese customs must be respected.

Leading Chinese formed the Po Leung Kuk, not to oppose the custom of 'mui tsai', but to oppose the abuses which led to the kidnapping and selling of women and children. After discussion with this body, the Government in 1887 passed an Ordinance for the Better Protection of Women and Children. In 1893 the Po Leung Kuk occupied temporary premises and three years later a more permanent home was established. This organization did—and still does—very good work in helping women and children to return to their own homes, in finding husbands for the girls or securing their adoption into good homes. The practice of 'mui tsai' was not, however, declared illegal by the British Parliament until 1922 and it still persists to some extent in Hong Kong.

The period after the First World War, in Hong Kong as
in Britain, saw an increased interest in social welfare. A
beginning was made with factory legislation in 1923 when
an ordinance was passed which protected children working
in industry. Subsequently more and more ordinances were
passed dealing with working conditions in industry, and in
1938 a Labour Officer was appointed to deal with general
conditions of labour and the organization of trade unions.

This period also saw the growth of several voluntary
welfare organizations, some of them attached to Churches,
others not linked with any religious body. For instance, the
Society for the Protection of Children was started in 1929.
In 1938 the Social Service Centre of the Churches was set
up to expand case-work among the poor which had started
some time earlier. The work of this organization was restarted
after the war by the Social Welfare Council, which in 1949
developed into the Family Welfare Society.

In 1938 the sudden influx of refugees from China meant
that there was an increased need for social welfare work, so
the voluntary agencies set up an 'Emergency Relief Council'
which tried to co-ordinate the work of the various groups so
as to help the refugees more speedily.

SOCIAL WELFARE WORK SINCE THE SECOND WORLD WAR

The period since the Second World War has seen an even
greater expansion of social welfare work, both by the Government and by voluntary effort. The Government set up its
Social Welfare Office in 1948 as part of the Secretariat for
Chinese Affairs. Ten years later this became a full department,
the Department of Social Welfare. This change reflects the
greater importance given to such work.

This department is organized in six sections, each dealing
with a different group or different problem. One section is

concerned with child welfare, another with youth welfare, and a third with the welfare of women and girls. Then there is a Probation section which tries to guide delinquents into better habits of life. A Relief section is mainly engaged in the giving of outdoor relief, largely food, while the Special Welfare Services help the blind, the deaf, and others who are physically handicapped. In all this, the efforts of the Social Welfare Department are supplemented by the work of over a hundred voluntary welfare organizations and numerous smaller groups of people whose consciences are touched by the amount of distress in Hong Kong and who are eager to help those in need without destroying their self-respect. Most of these voluntary organizations have started since the end of the Second World War. Thus, though the Canossa Home started caring for blind children in 1863 and the Ebenezer Home for the Blind was established in 1897, the Hong Kong Society for the Blind was started only in 1955. The Society for the Relief of Disabled Children, the Boys' and Girls' Clubs Association, the Hong Kong Family Welfare Society, and many others are all post-war organizations.

Since 1949 there has been a considerable development of Kai Fong Associations, and twenty-eight of these neighbourhood groups now exist and give help in the fields of education, medicine and social welfare. Based as they are on the Chinese tradition of dwellers in the same street or district co-operating for mutual protection, the Kai Fongs might well play an important part in securing the active co-operation of the ordinary people of Hong Kong in the attempts being made to deal with the great social problems which exist in the Colony.

In addition to the welfare work done by the Department of Social Welfare and the voluntary societies, much allied work is done by other government departments such as the Resettlement Department, the Education Department, the Medical and Health Department and the Labour Department.

The social problems of Hong Kong are tremendous. Yet, though one cannot look forward optimistically to these problems being overcome, one can see that a greater effort than ever before is being made to relieve the worst distress. In this effort there is growing co-operation among different sections of the community, co-operation between the Government and the voluntary societies, co-operation among the Chinese, Europeans, Indians and others, co-operation among the various religious and secular agencies which are working at these problems. The Emergency Relief Council set up in 1938 has grown into the Hong Kong Council of Social Service, an organization which not only co-ordinates the efforts of the various societies but itself takes the lead in starting new projects.

THE LABOUR DEPARTMENT

The Labour Office has also expanded its work greatly. In 1946 it became a separate department and in the following year the head of the department became known as the Commissioner of Labour. With the rapid growth of new factories and the influx of people from the mainland who were eager for work whatever the conditions, there were many abuses reminiscent of the early days of the Industrial Revolution in England. Many abuses still flourish, but the efforts of the Labour Department with support from the Government in England, are improving labour conditions in all directions—hours of work, safety measures, health and welfare.

This period has also seen a growth in trade unions. A separate department, the Registry of Trade Unions, was set up in 1954 to register and to advise trade unions. Trade unions, however, remain generally weak, though they are slowly increasing in strength and gaining in efficiency.

Though the last decade has seen a very great growth in educational, medical and social welfare work in Hong Kong, this serves to show the need for still greater achievements.

Much more requires to be done, but there is now a greater awareness of the needs than ever before and a greater number of people who are eager to help bring about better conditions.

Extracts from Chadwick's Report on the Sanitation of Hong Kong to the Crown Agents for the Colonies.

18th July 1882.

Gentlemen,

I have the honour to submit herewith, for transmission to the Right Honourable the Secretary of State for the Colonies, the following Report on the Sanitary Condition of Hong Kong, together with suggestions for the improvement of such defects as in my opinion exist.

I proceeded to ascertain the feelings of the Chinese population, and to elicit information as to their domestic institutions, so that the measures proposed might be suited to them, and have as far as possible as a basis, time-honoured custom. . . .

Having thus obtained some knowledge of the sanitary habits and institutions of the people for whose benefit the measures are principally intended, I trust that my suggestions will prove satisfactory and practicable.

The principal objections raised, were due to fear of increased taxation, and to a dread of tyrannical interference by public officials, of 'squeeze', in short. In framing suggestions I have given special attention to the best means of avoiding these evils. . . .

The sanitary condition of Hong Kong is defective, and calls for energetic remedial measures. The death-rate is high, whilst the average age at death is low. . . .

The present water supply is inadequate, but this is about to be remedied. Unless waste of water be prevented, neither the proposed works, nor works many times larger, would satisfy the wants of the city. . . .

179

Both the design and construction of existing dwellings are defective—the Building Ordinance requires complete revision. The amended law must be enforced with more rigour and intelligence than at present, particularly as to alleys, lanes, and open spaces.

The system of house drainage is radically bad. The whole of the dwellings within the town require re-draining, and unless this is done but little health-improvement will be made.

The complete cheap and proper execution of this work can only be effected by the Government undertaking it. The cost will be considerable even if carried out with the greatest economy. . . . As the general public and the tenants are the principal beneficiaries by the expenditure for house improvement, it will be just and expedient for the Government to pay for their execution out of general revenue. . . .

As to scavenging and night-soil collection . . . the present bucket system must continue in an improved form. To this end the night-soil removal contract must be separated from that of street sweeping. The night-soil contractors should have the complete monopoly of that substance for which they would pay a large sum on account of its value; they would see that complete collection took place. In the end a system of water carriage will certainly prove most satisfactory, when all is ready for its gradual introduction. . . .

For the proper supervision of all these works, to introduce habits of cleanliness, to detect and remedy evils, an organized sanitary staff is required. . . .

I would call attention to the indifferent condition of the markets, and the want of baths for the poor, also public laundries. The second want was pointed out to me by the Tung-Wah Committee. The provision of a proper water supply for Kowloon Peninsula is recommended, also for some of the larger villages. . . .

I trust that even should these suggestions be found undesirable or impracticable, my report will show the necessity for strong and complete measures of sanitation, and I trust they will be undertaken for the immediate benefit of the public health, without waiting for the necessity to be demonstrated by the irresistible logic of a severe epidemic.

I have, &c.
(Signed) OSBERT CHADWICK,
Associate Member Inst. C.E.

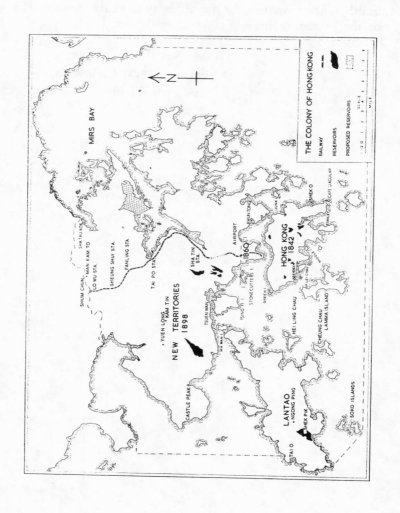

THE COLONY OF HONG KONG

CHAPTER XII

Chinese and Foreigners in Hong Kong

PRESENT FRIENDLINESS

Chinese and Europeans differ from each other in many ways; their food, their manner of eating, their social customs, the things that are polite in conversation, often differ. Yet today there is a good deal of mutual respect and much friendship between the two races in Hong Kong. They not only work together in business, in hospitals, in schools, in offices, but they often mix together outside their work, they play together, they visit each other, and more and more frequently they marry each other. The co-operation between them has not always been as happy as it often is now, and in many ways this close co-operation is very recent.

MUTUAL CONTEMPT IN THE NINETEENTH CENTURY

For quite a long time there was a basic antagonism between the Chinese and the Europeans, or perhaps a mutual contempt rather than antagonism. In the middle of the nineteenth century neither race knew much about the other. Few Chinese spoke any English, and those who did spoke it very imperfectly; not many Europeans spoke Chinese. A few learnt the language—Gutzlaff and Morrison, for instance— and their fame rests largely on the fact that they did master the language.

The Chinese felt certain that they were superior to the Europeans. They had an ancient civilization, and the fact that Europeans came so far to the shores of China was surely proof of Chinese superiority. The British, the chief of the Europeans to come to China, conscious of their growing achievements in industry, science and trade, were equally convinced of *their* own superiority. These attitudes did not make for friendly relations.

In fact the differences between the two races were so great that there was from the beginning of the occupation of Hong Kong an unofficial segregation. The Chinese preferred to live with their own people, folk of similar language and customs; the British, just as naturally, preferred to live in districts inhabited by their own people. Differing habits and customs made living apart quite natural.

LEGAL EQUALITY

At first, as we have seen in Chapter V, Captain Elliot showed himself eager to protect the interests of the Chinese in Hong Kong. They were promised that they would be governed according to the laws of China and would be allowed free exercise 'of their religious rites, ceremonies and social customs'. This system, Chinese law for the Chinese and British law for the Europeans, proved very difficult to administer properly, since the Chinese elders had little authority over those Chinese who came into the Colony. So in practice, law and order were maintained by the British officials, and seventeen years after the occupation of Hong Kong the dual system of Chinese law and British law was abandoned. The new principle was stated by H. Labouchère, the Secretary of State for the Colonies, in 1858. He stressed that there should be, as far as possible, 'uniformity of legislation for the several races inhabiting the colonial possessions of the Crown'. This principle was emphasized in 1866 when the instructions to the new Governor, Sir Richard Graves MacDonnell, forbade him to assent to any ordinance 'whereby persons of African or Asiatic birth may be subject to any disabilities or restrictions to which persons of European birth or descent are not also subjected', without the consent of the Home Government.

184

Hong Kong harbour

Various examples show that the British Government sincerely believed in legal equality. Thus in 1886 the Hong Kong Government passed a special ordinance against armed bands engaged in smuggling opium. By this ordinance all Chinese were forbidden to carry arms, except with the permission of the Governor-in-Council. Lord Stanhope, Secretary of State for the Colonies, insisted that the word 'persons' should be used instead of 'Chinese', so as to avoid any differentiation between the races.

A few years later, in 1895, another Secretary of State, Lord Ripon, refused to accept an ordinance restricting Chinese entry into Hong Kong in time of plague, since he felt that no ordinance should be directed against only one section of the community.

Two years after this, the Government removed a humiliating example of discrimination when it abolished the system whereby any Chinese out after 9 p.m. had to carry a special pass. This had been in force since 1843. In the early years, when many of the Chinese coming into the Colony were not particularly law-abiding, there might have been some excuse for this measure, but it had long caused great ill-feeling among many Chinese residents of Hong Kong.

ADMINISTRATIVE INEQUALITY

These illustrations show that official policy was based upon racial equality. In the administration of the laws, however, there was for a long time considerable discrimination. One bad example of this occurred in 1857. A European, Murrow, and five Chinese were found guilty of keeping 240 coolie emigrants imprisoned against their will while waiting for a ship; the Chinese were each sentenced to six months' imprisonment, while Murrow was simply fined five dollars! It is, however, interesting to note that this decision was sharply criticized in England. Complaints were also made from time to time about the readiness of the police to strike Chinese for minor or imagined breaches of the law. Such cases did not occur only in the middle of last century, and there are Chinese living in Hong Kong today who remember seeing such actions.

SOCIAL DISTINCTIONS

Discrimination showed itself most strongly in the social sphere. Social distinctions in Hong Kong were not based only on race but also, as elsewhere, on wealth, education and occupation. Such distinctions still exist, though with the spread of education and the development of ideas of equality they are now far less strong than before.

The chief social distinctions, however, divided Europeans and Chinese. This was due to several factors. The quality of the first Chinese who came to Hong Kong was not very high; some of them committed many crimes and they had, in most cases, come to gain what they could from the foreigners. At the same time the Europeans who arrived in Hong Kong did not always represent the best examples of European culture and behaviour. As already noted, the appalling ignorance of each other's culture, customs and language established a strong barrier between the races. As a result the two races did not mix socially. They met on business, they traded together, but then they separated. Outside business the main contact of Europeans with Chinese was with servants and workmen, while outside business the Chinese merchants had no contacts with Europeans at all.

Such voluntary segregation would break down only when representatives of the two races no longer felt strange with each other, when they had a language in which they could talk together, when they lost their strong racial pride and regarded each other as people rather than as representatives of different races. It took a long time for these barriers to be even partially broken down, and one of the main reasons for this was racial pride, the belief by men of each race that they were superior. There was on each side, as we have seen, some good reason for this feeling; the wide differences between the two traditions prevented a quick appreciation of each other's virtues. These facts led the European minority, the ruling race, to treat the Chinese majority with contempt, feeling that the latter were inferior.

This attitude began to change a little when the T'ai P'ing rebellion led to a large influx of Chinese, many of whom were well-educated men of means. The eventual breaking down of this feeling, however, would only come when the leaders of the community—particularly the Governors—deliberately tried to bring about closer contacts between the races, and when through education the two races began to gain understanding of each other.

ATTITUDES OF BOWRING AND ROBINSON

Bowring in 1858 was distressed by the fact that 'the separation of the native population from the European is nearly absolute; social intercourse between the races wholly unknown', but he did nothing to improve matters. His successor, Sir Hercules Robinson, apparently thought that such segregation was a good thing. In 1861 he wrote to the Secretary of State for the Colonies about the Chinese population in Kowloon, showing himself concerned about 'how best to keep them to themselves and preserve the European and American community from the injury and inconvenience of intermixture with them'. This hints at one of the difficulties of the peoples living close together. There was a great difference in standards of sanitation between the wealthier Europeans and the poorer Chinese—just as there was in England between the wealthy and the poor. So the Europeans wished to keep away from the crowded and often dirty and unhealthy areas where most of the Chinese lived.

Kennedy (1872–7) showed himself ready to try to bridge the gap between the two races. He showed great friendliness towards the Chinese and was the first Governor to invite some of them to functions at Government House. This at least was an official beginning to inter-racial mingling outside the office or warehouse, but it was no more than a beginning. Things got better as education in English began to spread in the Colony and especially as Chinese students studied abroad and then returned to Hong Kong. Between such students and the foreigners there was a common language, English, and moreover such Chinese had a greater knowledge and understanding of the Western way of life than their fathers had. This meant, however, that the contacts between Chinese and Europeans were usually made as a result of the Chinese studying English and learning about the West, rather than as a result of European efforts to learn Chinese and to understand the Chinese people and culture. This has been largely true down to the present. Many of the foreigners living in Hong Kong have very little knowledge of the Chinese and know only those who have received a Western education.

IMPROVEMENT UNDER HENNESSY

The spread of some degree of European education among a few of the Chinese made it possible for them to be given responsible posts in the administration. Thus the admission of Chinese to the Legislative Council, started by Hennessy, helped to raise the status of the whole Chinese community. This in turn helped to make social contacts somewhat easier and less unusual.

Hennessy opposed all discrimination against Chinese. He opened the lower government posts to competition, and he maintained that Chinese government employees should be given pensions as were the Europeans, and not just gratuities. He also opposed racial discrimination in the use of the City

Hall which had been opened in 1869. The committee had decided to restrict the use of the museum and library to Europeans on Sundays and at certain hours on weekdays, and to Chinese women on one morning a week. Hennessy greatly annoyed many Europeans by threatening to withdraw the government grant if this rule was not withdrawn.

THE CHINESE BEGIN TO SETTLE IN THE CENTRAL DISTRICT

Nevertheless there was very little real social contact between Europeans and Chinese and they continued to live in different districts. In the 1870s Chinese firms were taking over a larger proportion of the Colony's trade and began to settle in the Central District which had hitherto been a European preserve. This was not illegal, though there were restrictions on the building of Chinese-type houses and shops.

Hennessy supported the Chinese merchants. In 1877, 'It being a matter of principal importance that no obstruction should be put in the way of the natural course of trade', it was agreed that 'permits be freely granted for native structures along any part of Queen's Road, and business streets immediately adjoining', to a line joining Upper Wyndham Street, Hollywood Road and Aberdeen Street. This policy was not agreed upon without opposition from some of the chief officials of the Government. The following year Hennessy reported, 'One sees warehouses that a few years ago were in the midst of a European district . . . now in the occupation of the Chinese.'

EUROPEAN RESERVATIONS

Partly because they felt the Chinese population was less sanitary than they and more likely to spread disease, many Europeans now demanded that certain districts be reserved for European residence. As we have seen, there had been separate residential districts for Europeans but, with the growth of the Chinese population and of Chinese prosperity, these districts were being invaded. In 1888 a European Reservation Ordinance created a European reservation in the Caine Road district. Legally this was not a question of racial segregation for only the type of housing was restricted, but in effect it did preserve this area for European residence.

After the discovery that malaria was spread by mosquitoes, Europeans again demanded that there should be special residential areas for Europeans, on the grounds that the Chinese would not take precautions against the breeding of mosquitoes. In 1902 a sub-committee of the Sanitary Board proposed to reserve an area of about 20,000 acres in Kowloon, between Tsim Sha Tsui and Kowloon City, for Europeans. The reasons given for this were to ensure proper malarial control and to keep down the rents which would go up if rich Chinese wanted to live there. Chamberlain, the Secretary of State for the Colonies, agreed with the first reason but had no sympathy with the second, so it was decided that the district should be thrown open to all persons approved by the Governor. In 1904 the Peak District was reserved on the same conditions. In effect, though not in law, these reservations were for the use of Europeans.

MUTUAL CONTEMPT REMAINED

In the attitudes of the two races to one another the old feelings of contempt continued to exist, though there was little real hostility and some close friendships. In 1895 Granville Sharp, in a public speech, mentioned that 'years ago, all coolies doffed their caps and stood on one side; now they don't'. Yet this suggests that to a large extent the feeling concerned class rather than race, for the same sort of remark was being made in England with regard to the lower classes.

One added difficulty in achieving good relations between Chinese and Europeans was the constantly changing population. Europeans came and went; Chinese came and went.

There were always large numbers of newcomers who had to overcome their prejudices against each other; before they had reached a true respect for each other's good points and a toleration of each other's weak points, they moved away from the Colony, back to China or back to Europe.

RELIGION HELPS TO OVERCOME RACIAL PREJUDICE

We have mentioned the spread of European education among the Chinese as one of the important steps which contributed towards greater friendship between Chinese and Europeans. We must also mention the religious activities of the missionaries. Chinese Christians tended, and still tend, to be closer to Europeans than most other Chinese. A common religion helped to lead to closer friendships between men of different races.

Yet despite education and missionary endeavour and the attitude of a Governor like Hennessy, there was still very little social contact between the races even at the beginning of this century. There were close individual friendships but not many of them. The outbreak of the Boxer rebellion in 1900 did not improve mutual trust but led to an increase of suspicion between the races.

IMPROVEMENTS IN SOCIAL RELATIONS SINCE 1911

The years following the Chinese Revolution in 1911 led to a growth of anti-foreign feeling among the Chinese because of the resentment at the privileges held by foreign governments in China. Yet social relations improved. This was partly because more Chinese had been abroad for their education or had received higher education in the University of Hong Kong, and found themselves able to mix more freely with Europeans. It was partly also because China was now actively learning much from the West and was beginning to relax its former attitude of superiority. At the same time the Westerners, particularly after the fierce struggle of the

Tai Hang Tung resettlement estate

First World War, were less certain of their own superiority. An important contribution to the growth of mutual understanding was made by the growing Eurasian community.

Prejudice still continued, however, and one extreme example of it is shown in a letter to the *China Mail* in May 1922, during a ferry strike which led to curtailed ferry services and consequent overcrowding. The writer, who signed himself 'Paterfamilias', said angrily, '. . . European ladies ought to be given first chance of getting a seat and the Chinese allowed on afterwards, if there is room. . . . At least it should be seen to that the Chinese are restricted to the third class section of the ferries'.

This letter was answered by a Chinese who, writing under the name 'Critic', chided 'Paterfamilias' for his narrow-mindedness and then went on, with his tongue in his cheek: 'Foreigners should be given only third class seats, and the Chinese be given the first class ones. How would the foreigners like this? "Paterfamilias", be more sensitive than this, and you shall enjoy the friendship of the natives here'.

Nevertheless prejudices were slowly disappearing and there were various indications of the changing attitude. In 1926, for instance, Chinese were for the first time admitted as members of the Jockey Club. Gradually, too, Chinese in Hong Kong began to adopt more and more Western pursuits, football, swimming, dancing, going to the cinema; more and more of them began to adopt Western dress. On the other hand, more Europeans showed a desire to learn about China and the Chinese, and so the races began to move a little closer together.

This process has been accelerated since the end of the Second World War. Where segregation now exists it is largely due to economic factors rather than to race; there are some areas where few, if any, Europeans live and others, though fewer, where few Chinese live, but there is no segregation of housing as such. There are still examples of racial prejudice by men of both races, still some clubs which are racially exclusive, but few people now would admit to a belief in their own racial superiority. It is noticeable too, that a beginning has been made to abolish race distinctions in regard to salary scales. For example, in the Hong Kong Government service expatriation allowances, normally payable to staff recruited from overseas, have been abolished in the case of some of the higher grades of the Civil Service in accordance with the recommendations of the Salaries Commission Report of 1958.

In Hong Kong there are huge economic differences, there are various linguistic groups and there are many groups whose habits, customs and religions differ widely. Despite these differences, however, racial relationships are generally good and are improving, and certainly at no other time in the history of Hong Kong have they been better. If life in Hong Kong leads to the development of mutual respect and understanding among the races who live here, then the Colony has an importance greater than that which comes from its trade and industry.

Extract from a speech to the Hong Kong Legislative Council, 3rd June 1881, by Sir John Pope Hennessy.

. . . I may, perhaps, take this opportunity of saying a few words upon a subject which has, no doubt, sometimes attracted your attention, and that is the allegation made that during the four years of my government of this Colony, I have too much encouraged the Chinese. Now, I believe that the duty of a Governor in dealing with a community such as I find here, is to avoid what is popularly called encouragement of any body, or of any class, but to simply hold the balance evenly between all men. And that is what I have done. Coming here with a few years' experience, at the other side of the China Sea, of the Government of a Chinese community, I very soon after my arrival was waited on by some Chinese gentlemen of Hong Kong, who frankly told me their position in the Colony. They pointed out to me that there were certain restrictions, some laid upon them, others attempted to be laid upon them, to which they objected, and they asked me, at all events, to assist them to this extent—not to allow undue or unfair restrictions to be laid on the Chinese, but to give them that same equality and fair play that they thought they were entitled to with all other subjects of the Queen.

Well, gentlemen, it is upon such questions as these that I have been able to give to the Chinese community positive assurances to the effect that I would make no distinction between them and the other British subjects in the Colony. The mere fact of doing that which was, after all, but a negative exercise of the functions of the Government has gained for the Government the confidence of the Chinese Community, and they have come to the Colony for the last three years in large numbers. They are settling here, buying property, and what they are doing is, no doubt, of great interest to us all.

I must say it is of interest to me as the Queen's Representative, not merely because I see Her Majesty's Chinese subjects prosperous, but because what is going on in Hong Kong tends to render prosperous men of our own race from England, Scotland and Ireland in this Colony. I rejoice, also, to see that this prosperity is shared in by the Armenians, the Parsees, and other subjects of the Empress of India, as well as by the Portuguese, the Americans, the Frenchmen, the Germans, and the other foreigners who have enjoyed the commercial advantages of an Anglo-Chinese Colony and the protection of the British flag. . . .

The Story of Macao

The Portuguese settlement of Macao occupies a small peninsula lying at the most southerly point on the western side of the Pearl River estuary, opposite Hong Kong which occupies a corresponding position forty-six miles across the estuary to the east. Macao is much older than Hong Kong, for the Portuguese were the first European seafarers to come to the China Coast in search of trade. Macao in fact has over four hundred years of history.

THE PORTUGUESE REACH CHINA

When Albuquerque, an intrepid Portuguese commander, captured Malacca in 1511, he made friends with some Chinese traders who frequented that port in their large junks, with the result that Portuguese pioneering voyages were organized to the South China Coast, as early as 1513-5. In 1516, Rafael Perestrello was sent to try to establish commercial contacts. In the next year, Fernao Peres de Andrade arrived in command of a trading fleet of eight junks, two of which he was allowed to take up the river to Canton to open Western trade with China. Two years later, in 1519, Tomé Pires was sent on an embassy to Peking, but unfortunately for him, Simao de Andrade, who had arrived with four ships, angered the Chinese by trying to capture Chinese trading junks. Pires was sent back to Canton by the Emperor as a prisoner and died in prison there. The Portuguese were barred from the Canton area for the next thirty years, and so they tried to establish themselves farther north, in Chekiang Province and Chinchew.

In 1543 Japan was accidentally discovered by some Portuguese deserters sailing in a junk, and this led to the development of a highly profitable trade with that country. There were two chief reasons why the trade was profitable. Trade between China and Japan had been forbidden by the Ming Emperors, so the Portuguese acted as carriers between the two countries; as Chinese silk was more valuable in Japan, and the silver which the Japanese paid in exchange was more valuable in China, the Portuguese reaped a rich reward each way. Secondly, the Portuguese had no competitors in carrying goods between Europe, India, the East Indies and China and Japan. It was no wonder then that the Portuguese regarded this trade with Japan as extremely valuable. A Chinese port of call for refitting ships, drying cargo and taking on water and stores was essential for ships making the long voyage from Goa or Malacca to Japan. When the Portuguese settlements at Chekiang and Chinchew were destroyed in 1545 and 1549, the Portuguese began to establish contacts on some islands in the Canton area, particularly on St. John's Island or San Ch'uan 上川, some fifty miles south-west of Macao. It was to this island that St. Francis Xavier, the great Christian missionary to Japan, was brought in 1552 on his fatal illness. A settlement was also made on Lampacao, nearer Macao. There was no annexation or treaty, and probably no permanent settlement, and separate arrangements were usually made on each voyage by a Portuguese official called 'the Captain-Major of the Japan Voyage', who was a prominent Portuguese merchant to whom the monopoly of the trade with Japan had been sold. An annual fair or exhibition of articles of Portuguese trade, held on one or other of the two islands mentioned, led inevitably to the need for more permanent arrangements and Macao came into being as a Portuguese settlement in 1557.

The exact conditions under which the Portuguese were allowed to reside in Macao are not known, and they were probably a purely local arrangement between the Canton mandarins and the Portuguese Captain-Major. Macao was not at first recognized as a Portuguese colony or settlement by either the Portuguese or the Chinese Governments or by the Portuguese authorities in Goa. The explanation usually given is that the Chinese granted the Portuguese the right of residence in Macao as a reward for successful attacks against local pirates. In any case, Macao was more convenient than the islands of St. John and Lampacao which the Portuguese had been using for some time, because its harbour was more sheltered and it was so much closer to the great trading centre of Canton.

The name Macao is almost certainly derived from Amangao, or Ama-go, the Bay of the goddess Ama, whose temple was already there and is still to be found today. The Portuguese called it 'The Settlement of the Name of God in China', and then in 1586 as the Settlement grew, 'The City of the Name of God in China'; but this was too cumbersome and the name Macao or Macau became attached to it and has remained in general use ever since. In its early days, Macao was controlled by the Captain-Major of the Japan Voyage, but in 1586, the new settlement was recognized by the Portuguese authorities in Goa, and allowed to have its own Senate composed of three citizens elected indirectly and three officials, with the Captain-Major's control limited to the garrison.

Chinese residents whom the settlement later attracted were controlled by a Chinese magistrate and the Portuguese paid an annual ground rent of 500 taels. It was a practical and workable arrangement made by practical people without regard to legal niceties, and it suited both Chinese and Portuguese that they should live according to their own laws, under their own officials.

THE DUTCH THREAT

The Portuguese had to meet the attacks of the Dutch who were trying to take the Far Eastern trade from their control, and in 1622 Macao was attacked by a Dutch expedition which was repelled largely because of the explosion of a Dutch gunpowder wagon. The Dutch threat led to the appointment of a special officer called the Captain-General of Macao, who was to be in charge of the garrison. He acted as a kind of Governor of the settlement with power to make appointments, though he had to share control with the Senate which levied taxation and controlled the finances.

THE DECLINE OF MACAO

In 1639 the Portuguese trade with Japan came to an abrupt end, following the rise to power of the Tokugawa Shoguns which marked the beginning of the Tokugawa Seclusion. For the next two hundred years and more, Japan isolated itself almost completely from the rest of the world.

The great days of Macao were now over, for Japanese trade had been a vital factor in the origin, growth and prosperity of the settlement. In addition, the Dutch siege and conquest of Malacca in 1641 stopped communication with Goa for a time and Macao had to depend on itself. Macao remained an entrepôt for trade between China and the rest of the world, Europe, India, the East Indies and the Philippines, but by the eighteenth century it had decayed to a shadow of its former self. It also remained a centre of Christian missionary effort in China in which the Jesuits played a leading part. For one of the characteristics of the Portuguese expansion overseas was that they brought with them the Roman Catholic Faith and, actively and as a matter of official policy, supported the work of the Church, making Macao the great centre of European cultural as well as commercial contact with China.

Macao was the recognized port of call for all European maritime nations seeking to trade with China. John Weddell came in 1637 and attempted to trade directly with the Chinese at Canton; but when he met with Chinese resistance, he attempted to force his way up the Bogue* and finally had to seek the help of the Macao officials to induce the Chinese to liberate some of his men who had been captured ashore and held as hostages. The British made several attempts to trade with China but did not succeed in putting their trade on a satisfactory footing until the beginning of the eighteenth century.

The Portuguese naturally refused to allow any other nation to set up a 'factory' in Macao, but shipping went to Macao for refitting and provisioning after the long and arduous voyage through the China Sea. The British trade was under the control of the English East India Company, which tried to establish factories at Ningpo and Amoy, but after 1757 the Chinese restricted all trade with Europeans to Canton. Europeans were permitted to establish factories there, just beyond the city wall and fronting the river, but they were not allowed to reside except during the trading season, usually from October to May. At first the Company's trading officials returned to India with their vessels at the close of the season's trading, but as trade expanded they began to stay, and obtained permission to reside at Macao during the close season. Women were forbidden by the Chinese to live in the Canton factories, and so families had to reside in the Portuguese settlement all the year round.

So Macao played a vital part in the life of British and American and European traders. They leased fine houses there, and it became a social and recreational centre. The first English newspapers in China were printed there. The expansion of their Indian Empire helped the British to

---

* From the Portuguese Bocca Tigris ('tiger's mouth'), the entrance to the Pearl River.

capture most of the Western trade with China, and Macao suffered in consequence, yet it was Macao which performed the essential function of providing the British with a permanent footing in China. The East India Company's monopoly was abolished in 1833. Lord Napier arrived the following year in the post of Chief Superintendent of Trade, and when his mission was rejected it was to Macao that he returned. Macao remained the British administrative centre until the spring of 1842, by which time Hong Kong had been occupied.

THE CESSION OF MACAO TO PORTUGAL

The cession of Hong Kong naturally raised the question of the exact position of Macao, and the Portuguese made efforts to set up Macao as a free port and quite independent of China. But this led to the assassination of the Governor, Amaral, in 1849. It was not until 1887 that Portugal secured, by treaty with China, the cession of Macao as a Portuguese colony.

Macao has not grown like Hong Kong because the British became in the nineteenth century the dominant commercial and overseas trading nation, and Hong Kong merchants captured the Canton trade. A second reason is that the harbour at Macao silted up and became too shallow for ocean-going ships of any large size. The Praya Grande, which used to be the commercial water-front, is now a government and residential area, and shipping is forced to use the inner harbour on the west side of the peninsula that constitutes Macao. In the absence of deep-water facilities, Macao was quite unable to meet the needs of the modern age. In its four hundred years of history it is not surprising that it has had both good times and lean times.

THE HISTORICAL INTEREST OF MACAO

Certainly Macao has much to interest the historian. Standing on the highest point is the old Guia Fort and Chapel dating back to 1626, and the lighthouse, one of the first on the China Coast, erected in 1864. In the centre of the city is the Leal Senado, formerly the seat of government, but now the Town Hall and Library; this building and its furniture date only from 1874, but are typically Portuguese in style. The Camoens Gardens and Grotto are traditionally associated with the great Portuguese poet Camoens, who is said to have written part of *The Lusiads* there. Nearby are the English Chapel and Cemetery, formerly belonging to the English East India Company, dating from 1821. The ruins of St. Paul's Church are most imposing; this Jesuit Church was built by Japanese Christians between 1594 and 1602. Its beautiful facade and stone steps, added some years later, were all that remained after the Church was destroyed by fire in 1834. The Monte Fort, first built by the Jesuits, adjoins the ruins. The Kun Yam Temple, dedicated to the Goddess of Mercy, existed before the Portuguese came, and is famous as the place at which the first treaty between China and the United States was signed in 1844. The Praya Grande, facing the sea, which used to be the commercial centre, still has a magnificent sweep to remind one of the past glories of Macao.

Places of Historical Interest in Hong Kong*

1. GOVERNMENT HOUSE

The first Government House, occupied by Sir Henry Pottinger, was situated on a site adjoining St. John's Cathedral, on which the offices of the Education Department now stand. The present Government House, between Upper and Lower Albert Roads, was completed in 1855. Some alterations, including the tower, were made by the Japanese during their occupation of Hong Kong.

2. THE CENTRAL GOVERNMENT OFFICES

These are very modern buildings in Lower Albert Road, but the site is one on which government offices have stood since the earliest days of the Colony. The old government offices, known as the Colonial Secretariat Building, which was pulled down in 1953 to make room for the east wing and central block of the new offices, dated from 1847. A bronze circular plaque, which can now be seen on the wall in the main entrance, commemorates the laying of the foundation stone of the old building by Sir John Davis, Bart. on 24th February 1847.

3. OLD CHINESE CANNON

At the Central Government Offices will also be found an old Chinese cannon. A Chinese inscription gives its history, showing that it was cast in the seventeenth century.

* Many of these are on private property and cannot ordinarily be visited.

4. MURRAY PARADE GROUND AND THE CRICKET GROUND

These are historic sites, as old as the Colony itself. The east side of Garden Road was a military area from the first, and the slope on the other side of the road was levelled to make the Murray Parade Ground, which was sold in 1961 as a building site. The cutting can be seen just below St. John's Cathedral. The sea then came up almost to Queen's Road at that point, and the cricket ground was made from the soil taken from the Murray Parade Ground.

5. MURRAY BARRACKS

The building at the corner of Garden Road and Queen's Road, part of Murray Barracks, is probably nearly as old as the Colony, for it is a feature of pictures of early Hong Kong. Flagstaff House, the official residence of the Commander British Forces, one of the oldest buildings in Hong Kong, dates from 1845.

6. ST. JOHN'S CATHEDRAL

The nave was completed in 1849 and the tower added three years later, but an intended spire has never been built. An enlarged chancel was built in 1869, and a commemoration stone with this date can be seen on the outside wall facing Garden Road. The Coat of Arms of Sir John Davis can be seen on the north side of the Tower, just over the porch.

7. THE BISHOP'S HOUSE

This house, situated in Lower Albert Road, bears the date 1851 and is one of the oldest surviving buildings in the Colony. It was intended also to serve as St. Paul's College.

8. THE COLONIAL CEMETERY, HAPPY VALLEY

This area has been in use as a cemetery since 1843, and the small mortuary chapel there dates from 1845, though it has been much restored.

9. JARDINE, MATHESON & COMPANY'S GODOWN

The remains of the old premises of Jardine, Matheson & Company at East Point contained until 1959 one old godown dating from 1843. The site, now very much built upon, was one of the earliest in Hong Kong to be occupied.

The tradition of firing a gun at midday is still observed by Jardine, Matheson & Company at East Point, though the old gun was lost during the Japanese occupation. The origin of the tradition is doubtful but one version is that one of the partners of the 'Princely Hong' was welcomed back from England with a salute of guns reserved for high officials of the State, and the firm was ordered to fire the daily gun as a punishment.

10. QUEEN'S ROAD

This was the first road constructed in Hong Kong. Its chief historic interest lies in the fact that it followed closely the line of the sea.

11. THE VICTORIA GAOL, CENTRAL MAGISTRACY AND THE CENTRAL POLICE STATION

These buildings, lying between Old Bailey Street and Hollywood Road, occupy a site used for police and prison purposes since 1842.

12. KELLETT ISLAND

This island was named after Captain H. Kellett, who commanded the survey ship *Starling* during the hostilities of 1840–2. Now joined to the mainland by a causeway, it was at first used by the British as the site of a fort, but only for a short time. What may possibly be part of the old fortress wall with slit windows can still be seen from the harbour side.

13. MILITARY CAMP AND CEMETERY AT STANLEY

An early military camp was established at Stanley, on the narrow neck of land now occupied by St. Stephen's College. The cemetery nearby still contains graves of British soldiers and families, many of them infants, some dating from the 1840s.

14. SAI WAN MILITARY CAMP

This again was a very early military camp. The old military citadel at the top of the hill is still a conspicuous landmark.

15. MILE POST AT TAI TAM RESERVOIR

The old road to Stanley followed the Wong Nei Chong valley to Wong Nei Chong Gap and then turned left to the Tai Tam Reservoir. Just across the reservoir and just before the steep descent to the lower Tai Tam Reservoirs, a bit of the old road is still to be seen, and a mile stone, similar to those used in Victorian England, by the side of the road. It is of granite, about four feet high. On one face is the inscription 'Victoria 5 miles', and on the other face 'Stanley' and the word 'miles', but the figure has been lost through weathering. The distance to Stanley is about 4 miles. The Chinese characters which follow in each case can only be read with great difficulty. The mile post is assumed to date from about 1847, the date of the road.

16. THE CONDUIT FROM POKFULAM RESERVOIR TO CONDUIT ROAD

The first reservoir, that at Pokfulam, was connected to filter beds above the town by a conduit. This was first built in 1864 and was subsequently reconstructed to form the present conduit which makes a pleasant walk of about three miles.

17. BELCHER FORT

There is very little left of this old military area in Sai Ying Poon, but the levelled area of the old Belcher Fort, on which Belcher Gardens now stand, can be seen, and also entrances to underground stores in the road below.

18. MEMORIAL STONE IN CHATER ROAD

This stone is to be found in the wall adjoining the Hong Kong Cricket Club ground. The inscription records that it was laid by the Duke of Connaught on 2nd April 1890, in commemoration of the commencement of the Praya Reclamation Works. This refers to the reclamation of the land on which Des Voeux, Connaught and Chater Roads now stand.

19. THE BOTANICAL GARDENS

These are situated on the slope just above Government House, and were the result of the enthusiasm of Sir John Bowring under whom they were begun in 1856.

20. THE ROMAN CATHOLIC CATHEDRAL

This lies just above Caine Road, adjoining the Botanical Gardens. The foundation stone was laid in 1884 and it was dedicated in 1888 as the Cathedral of the Immaculate Conception.

21. SCHOOL BUILDINGS

Of old school buildings which still exist (1961) two may be mentioned. There is the old St. Joseph's College, now Raimondi College, in Robinson Road, just above the Catholic Cathedral, continuously in use since 1882. The Church Missionary Society Day School in Hollywood Road which was in use as a school from 1876 to 1958, still stands; inside is a wall tablet to the memory of Harriet Baxter, founder of the Female Education Society, who worked for the education of girls in Hong Kong from 1860 to her death in 1865.

22. MONUMENTS IN HAPPY VALLEY

A small granite obelisk, situated at the junction of Queen's Road East, Wongneichong Road and Leighton Road, was erected in March 1847, by Captain Charles Talbot, the officers and crew of H.M.S. *Vestal* in memory of their shipmates who died whilst serving in the Far East.

A second small granite obelisk, a short distance away at the junction of Morrison Hill Road and Leighton Road, was erected by the officers and crew of the U.S. frigate *Powhatan* and H.M. steam sloop *Rattler* in memory of their shipmates who fell in a combined boat attack on a fleet of piratical junks off Kuhlan on 11th August 1855.

23. THE TOMB AT LI CHENG UK

The most ancient historical remains in the Colony is the Tomb, probably dating from the Han dynasty, found at Li Cheng Uk in 1955 and which all should visit.

24. THE SUNG WONG T'OI

This was a large granite boulder overlooking the old village of Ma Tau Chung, on which were inscribed three Chinese characters commemorating the refuge in Kowloon of the last boy Emperor of the Sung dynasty after his defeat by the Mongols in 1279. Part of the hill on which it stood was excavated by the Japanese during the Second World War and blasting begun on the rock in order to enlarge the airfield. A fragment of the Sung Wong T'oi is now placed near its original site in a specially laid-out enclosure. (Picture on page 51.)

25. KOWLOON CITY

The old walled city is now merged with Kowloon and the walls destroyed. In the picture on page 39, it is possible to see the site of the old city.

26. THE MONUMENT AT THE JUNCTION OF GASCOIGNE AND JORDAN ROADS

This was erected by the British community in Hong Kong to the memory of five French sailors, members of the crew of the French destroyer *Fronde*, who were lost during the 1906 typhoon. The inscriptions are in English and French.

27. BOUNDARY STREET, KOWLOON

This street is of historic interest as being the boundary of the Colony which was arranged in 1860, hence its name.

28. KAM TIN WALLED VILLAGE

This is interesting as a good example in the New Territories of a Chinese walled city; it dates probably from the time of the entry of the Puntis into the area at the time of the Ming dynasty. (Picture on page 84.)

29. SAN TIN

This city, to the north of Kam Tin, is interesting for its temple in which old clan tablets are preserved.

30. BOUNDARY STONES AT SHA TAU KOK

These are fixed in the middle of the main street at Sha Tau Kok to mark the boundary between China and the Leased Territory, 1899. British and Chinese negotiators each claimed Sha Tau Kok and the solution adopted was to divide it between the two, with the boundary running in the middle of the main street. (Picture on page 43.)

31. OLD CHINESE FORT AT TUNG CHUNG, LANTAO ISLAND

This old fort is well worth seeing and probably dates from the seventeenth century as part of the fortifications to protect the Pearl Estuary. In the late eighteenth or early nineteenth century it was occupied by the notorious pirate, Cheung Po Tsai. The guns are of different dates, and an inscription on one gun may be translated 'This gun weighs one thousand catties and was made in August in the fourteenth year of Cha Ching by Man Sui Lo'. This puts its date at 1809.

32. WATER-POLICE STATION AT TSIM SHA TSUI

This was built in 1884 and is a good example of the colonial architecture of that period.

33. MAN MO TEMPLE IN HOLLYWOOD ROAD

The name literally means 'Literary and Martial Valour Temple', from the names of the two deities worshipped there, Man Cheung Tai Tei, an official of the Chin dynasty honoured by Taoists as the God of literacy, and Kwan Shing Tei, a famous Han dynasty general. The date of the temple is unknown. The two sacred chairs for the two Gods were made in 1862 and 1885 and are well preserved.

34. BUDDHIST MONASTERY AT CASTLE PEAK

This is the oldest Buddhist monastic foundation in the Colony and is said to have been founded in 428 A.D. by Pei Tu 杯度, a legendary figure to whom many miraculous deeds are ascribed. A statue of Pei Tu dating from the tenth century is still to be seen. The present building dates from the mid-nineteenth century when the Taoists took over the monastery; it reverted to Buddhism in 1918.

The Governors of Hong Kong

Captain Charles Elliot	Administrator	
	January–August 1841	
Sir Henry Pottinger	Administrator	
	August 1841–June 1843	
	Governor	
	June 1843–May 1844	
Sir John Davis		1844–1848
Sir George Bonham		1848–1854
Sir John Bowring		1854–1859
Sir Hercules Robinson		1859–1865
W. T. Mercer	(Administered)	1865–1866
Sir Richard Graves MacDonnell		1866–1872
Sir Arthur Kennedy		1872–1877
Sir John Pope Hennessy		1877–1882
W. H. Marsh	(Administered)	1882–1883
Sir George Bowen		1883–1885
W. H. Marsh	(Administered)	1885–1887
Major-General Cameron	(Administered)	1887
Sir William Des Voeux		1887–1891
Major-General Digby Barker	(Administered)	1891
Sir William Robinson		1891–1898
Major-General W. Black	(Administered)	1898
Sir Henry Blake		1898–1903
F. H. May	(Administered)	1903–1904
Sir Matthew Nathan		1904–1907
Sir Frederick Lugard		1907–1912
Sir Francis May		1912–1919

Sir Reginald Stubbs	1919–1925
Sir Cecil Clementi	1925–1930
Sir William Peel	1930–1935
Sir Andrew Caldecott	1935–1937
Sir Geoffrey Northcote	1937–1940
Sir Mark Young	1941–1947
Sir Alexander Grantham	1947–1957
Sir Robert Black	1958–

Suggestions for further reading

Braga, J. M. (ed.)   *Hong Kong Business Symposium* (Hong Kong, 1957).

Collins, Sir Charles *Public Administration in Hong Kong* (London, 1952).

Eitel, E. J.   *Europe in China:* The History of Hong Kong from the beginning to the year 1882 (London and Hong Kong, 1895).

Endacott, G. B.   *A History of Hong Kong* (London, 1958).

Endacott, G. B. and She, Mrs. D. E.   *The Diocese of Victoria* (Hong Kong, 1949).

Harrison, B. (ed.)   *University of Hong Kong: The first fifty years, 1911–1961* (Hong Kong, 1962).
Hong Kong Government Annual Reports.

Ingrams, Harold   *Hong Kong* (London, 1952).

Orange, James   *The Chater Collection* (London, 1924).

Pennell, W. V.   *History of the Hong Kong General Chamber of Commerce, 1861–1961* (Hong Kong, 1961).

Sayer, G. R.   *Hong Kong, Birth, Adolescence and Coming of Age* (Oxford, 1937).

Stericker, J. and V.   *Hong Kong in Picture and Story*, (Hong Kong, 1953).

Szczepanik, Edward   *The Economic Growth of Hong Kong* (London, 1958).

Tregear T. R. and Berry, L.   *The Development of Hong Kong and Kowloon as Told in Maps* (Hong Kong, 1959).

Wright, A. (ed.)   *Twentieth Century Impressions of Hong Kong, Shanghai and Other Treaty Ports of China* (London, 1908).

Index

216